TEACHER'S PET PUBLICATIONS

PUZZLE PACK
for
Wuthering Heights

based on the book by
Emily Brontë

Written by
Mary B. Collins

© 2005 Teacher's Pet Publications
All Rights Reserved

The materials in this packet are copyrighted
by Teacher's Pet Publications, Inc.

These pages may be duplicated by the purchaser
for use in the purchaser's own classroom.

Copying any of these materials and distributing them
for any other purpose is a violation of the copyright laws.

© 2005 Teacher's Pet Publications, Inc.
www.tpet.com

INTRODUCTION
If you already own the LitPlan for this title, this Puzzle Pack will refresh your Unit Resource Materials and Vocabulary Resource Materials sections plus give you additional materials you can substitute into the tests. If you do not already have a complete LitPlan, these pages will give you some supplemental materials to use with your own plan. There are two main groups of materials: one set for unit words (such as characters' names, symbols, places, etc.) and one set for vocabulary words associated with the book.

WORD LIST
There is a word list for both the unit words and the vocabulary words. These lists show you which words are being used in the materials and the clues or definitions being used for those words. You may want to give students a word list with clues/definitions to help them, or you may want students to only have a word list (without clues/definitions) if you want them to work a little harder. Both are available for duplication. The word lists can also be your "calling key" for the bingo games.

FILL IN THE BLANK AND MATCHING
There are 4 each of the fill in the blank and matching worksheets for both the unit and vocabulary words. These pages can be used either as extra worksheets for students or as objective parts of a unit test. They can be done individually if students need extra help or as a whole class activity to review the material covered.

MAGIC SQUARES
The magic squares not only reinforce the material covered but also work on reasoning and math skills. Many teachers have told us that their students really enjoy doing these!

WORD SEARCH PUZZLES
The word search words go in all directions, as indicated on your answer keys. Two of the word search puzzles have the clues listed rather than the words. This makes the puzzle a little more difficult, but it reinforces the material better. Two word search puzzles have words only for students who find the clue puzzles too difficult.

CROSSWORD PUZZLES
Both unit and vocabulary word sections have 4 crossword puzzles.

BINGO CARDS
There are 32 individual bingo cards for the unit words and 32 individual bingo cards for the vocabulary words. You can use your word list as a "call list," calling the words at random and marking them off of your list as you go, or you could use the flash cards by cutting them apart and drawing the words at random from a hat (or box or whatever). To make a better review, you might ask for the definition and spelling of each word as you call it out–or you could call out the definitions and have students tell you the words they need to look for on the puzzle.

JUGGLE LETTERS
The vocabulary juggle letter game is intended to help students learn the spellings of the words. One sheet has the definitions listed on it as an extra help for students who need it or to reinforce the definitions if you choose to do so.

FLASH CARDS
We've included a set of vocabulary flash cards you can duplicate, cut, and fold for your students. Some teachers make a few sets for general use by the class; others make a set for each student. Some teachers duplicate them for each student and have the students cut & fold their own. You can cut out just the words and put them in a hat, have each student pick out one word and write the definition and a sentence for that word. Students then swap words and papers, with the next student adding a sentence of his own under the last one. You can have students swap as many times as you like. Each time the student will read the sentences written prior to his own and then add a sentence. You can cut out the words and definitions separately and play "I Have; Who Has?" Each student in the room draws a word and definition. The first student says, "I have (the name of the word). Who has the definition?" The student with the definition reads it then says, "I have (the name of the vocabulary word she has). Who has the definition?" The round continues until all words and definitions have been given.

Wuthering Heights Word List

No.	Word	Clue/Definition
1.	APPLESAUCE	Heathcliff dumps this on Edgar
2.	BRONTE	Author
3.	CARDS	Gambling game Heathcliff and Hareton played
4.	CATHERINE	Mr. Earnshaw's daughter
5.	CATHY	Daughter of Edgar & Catherine
6.	COUSIN	Relationship of Cathy to Linton or Hareton
7.	CRY	Make tears; boo-hoo
8.	DREAM	Catherine appears to Lockwood in a ____
9.	EARNSHAW	He took in Heathcliff
10.	EDGAR	Catherine's Husband
11.	FIT	Catherine threw herself into one and locked herself in her room
12.	FRANCES	Hindley's wife
13.	GATE	Fence door
14.	GHOST	Heathcliff pleads for Catherine's to haunt him
15.	GRAVE	Final resting place
16.	GUN	Isabella warns Heathcliff that Hindley has one
17.	HARETON	Son of Hindley
18.	HEATHCLIFF	Revenge and Catherine are his passions
19.	HEIR	One who inherits
20.	HINDLEY	Catherine's brother
21.	ISABELLA	Heathcliff's wife
22.	JOSEPH	Self-righteous servant of Heathcliff
23.	KIDNAP	What Heathlciff did to Cathy and Nelly
24.	LETTERS	Nelly cuts these off between Cathy and Linton
25.	LINTON	Isabella or Edgar
26.	LOCK	Catherine ____ed her door & stayed in her room
27.	LOCKWOOD	He rented Thrushcross Grange
28.	LOVE	Feeling Catherine and Heathcliff have for each other
29.	MARRIAGE	What Heathcliff wants for Cathy & Linton
30.	MOOR	Meeting place for Cathy & Linton
31.	MORTGAGES	Heathcliff holds these on Wuthering Heights
32.	NELLY	____Dean; housekeeper
33.	PENISTON	____Crags
34.	PITY	Cathy's feelings for Linton
35.	PUPPIES	Hareton hangs a litter of these
36.	REVENGE	Heathcliff's specialty
37.	SERVANTS	Nelly, Joseph, and Zillah, for example
38.	SICKLY	Describes Linton
39.	SOLITUDE	Lockwood's reason for renting Thrushcross Grange
40.	SPANIEL	Isabella's kind of dog
41.	THRUSHCROSS	____Grange; Linton home estate
42.	WILD	Word to describe Hareton as a boy
43.	WUTHERING	____Heights
44.	ZILLAH	Replaced Nelly at Wuthering Heights

Wuthering Heights Fill In The Blank 1

_____
_____
_____
_____
_____
_____
_____
_____
_____
_____
_____
_____
_____
_____
_____
_____
_____
_____
_____
_____

1. Describes Linton
2. Heathcliff's specialty
3. Heathcliff dumps this on Edgar
4. ____Heights
5. One who inherits
6. Hindley's wife
7. Isabella warns Heathcliff that Hindley has one
8. Author
9. He rented Thrushcross Grange
10. Isabella or Edgar
11. Make tears; boo-hoo
12. Feeling Catherine and Heathcliff have for each other
13. Lockwood's reason for renting Thrushcross Grange
14. Final resting place
15. Catherine threw herself into one and locked herself in her room
16. ____Grange; Linton home estate
17. Catherine's brother
18. Catherine ___ed her door & stayed in her room
19. What Heathcliff wants for Cathy & Linton
20. Relationship of Cathy to Linton or Hareton

Wuthering Heights Fill In The Blank 1 Answer Key

SICKLY	1. Describes Linton
REVENGE	2. Heathcliff's specialty
APPLESAUCE	3. Heathcliff dumps this on Edgar
WUTHERING	4. ____Heights
HEIR	5. One who inherits
FRANCES	6. Hindley's wife
GUN	7. Isabella warns Heathcliff that Hindley has one
BRONTE	8. Author
LOCKWOOD	9. He rented Thrushcross Grange
LINTON	10. Isabella or Edgar
CRY	11. Make tears; boo-hoo
LOVE	12. Feeling Catherine and Heathcliff have for each other
SOLITUDE	13. Lockwood's reason for renting Thrushcross Grange
GRAVE	14. Final resting place
FIT	15. Catherine threw herself into one and locked herself in her room
THRUSHCROSS	16. ____Grange; Linton home estate
HINDLEY	17. Catherine's brother
LOCK	18. Catherine ___ed her door & stayed in her room
MARRIAGE	19. What Heathcliff wants for Cathy & Linton
COUSIN	20. Relationship of Cathy to Linton or Hareton

Wuthering Heights Fill In The Blank 2

_____ 1. Heathcliff pleads for Catherine's to haunt him

_____ 2. ____Heights

_____ 3. Relationship of Cathy to Linton or Hareton

_____ 4. Daughter of Edgar & Catherine

_____ 5. Catherine ___ed her door & stayed in her room

_____ 6. Hindley's wife

_____ 7. Isabella's kind of dog

_____ 8. Catherine's brother

_____ 9. Nelly, Joseph, and Zillah, for example

_____ 10. Son of Hindley

_____ 11. Heathcliff dumps this on Edgar

_____ 12. Heathcliff holds these on Wuthering Heights

_____ 13. ____Grange; Linton home estate

_____ 14. Heathcliff's wife

_____ 15. Meeting place for Cathy & Linton

_____ 16. Lockwood's reason for renting Thrushcross Grange

_____ 17. Isabella or Edgar

_____ 18. Word to describe Hareton as a boy

_____ 19. Feeling Catherine and Heathcliff have for each other

_____ 20. Final resting place

Wuthering Heights Fill In The Blank 2 Answer Key

GHOST	1. Heathcliff pleads for Catherine's to haunt him
WUTHERING	2. ____Heights
COUSIN	3. Relationship of Cathy to Linton or Hareton
CATHY	4. Daughter of Edgar & Catherine
LOCK	5. Catherine ___ed her door & stayed in her room
FRANCES	6. Hindley's wife
SPANIEL	7. Isabella's kind of dog
HINDLEY	8. Catherine's brother
SERVANTS	9. Nelly, Joseph, and Zillah, for example
HARETON	10. Son of Hindley
APPLESAUCE	11. Heathcliff dumps this on Edgar
MORTGAGES	12. Heathcliff holds these on Wuthering Heights
THRUSHCROSS	13. ____Grange; Linton home estate
ISABELLA	14. Heathcliff's wife
MOOR	15. Meeting place for Cathy & Linton
SOLITUDE	16. Lockwood's reason for renting Thrushcross Grange
LINTON	17. Isabella or Edgar
WILD	18. Word to describe Hareton as a boy
LOVE	19. Feeling Catherine and Heathcliff have for each other
GRAVE	20. Final resting place

Wuthering Heights Fill In The Blank 3

1. _____ Crags
2. Daughter of Edgar & Catherine
3. _____ Dean; housekeeper
4. Isabella or Edgar
5. Isabella warns Heathcliff that Hindley has one
6. Author
7. Heathcliff pleads for Catherine's to haunt him
8. Isabella's kind of dog
9. Fence door
10. Son of Hindley
11. Feeling Catherine and Heathcliff have for each other
12. Heathcliff's wife
13. Relationship of Cathy to Linton or Hareton
14. Nelly cuts these off between Cathy and Linton
15. Revenge and Catherine are his passions
16. Word to describe Hareton as a boy
17. Catherine appears to Lockwood in a _____
18. Mr. Earnshaw's daughter
19. Heathcliff holds these on Wuthering Heights
20. One who inherits

Wuthering Heights Fill In The Blank 3 Answer Key

PENISTON	1. ____Crags
CATHY	2. Daughter of Edgar & Catherine
NELLY	3. ____Dean; housekeeper
LINTON	4. Isabella or Edgar
GUN	5. Isabella warns Heathcliff that Hindley has one
BRONTE	6. Author
GHOST	7. Heathcliff pleads for Catherine's to haunt him
SPANIEL	8. Isabella's kind of dog
GATE	9. Fence door
HARETON	10. Son of Hindley
LOVE	11. Feeling Catherine and Heathcliff have for each other
ISABELLA	12. Heathcliff's wife
COUSIN	13. Relationship of Cathy to Linton or Hareton
LETTERS	14. Nelly cuts these off between Cathy and Linton
HEATHCLIFF	15. Revenge and Catherine are his passions
WILD	16. Word to describe Hareton as a boy
DREAM	17. Catherine appears to Lockwood in a ____
CATHERINE	18. Mr. Earnshaw's daughter
MORTGAGES	19. Heathcliff holds these on Wuthering Heights
HEIR	20. One who inherits

Wuthering Heights Fill In The Blank 4

_____

_____

_____

_____

_____

_____

_____

_____

_____

_____

_____

_____

_____

_____

_____

_____

_____

_____

_____

_____

1. Daughter of Edgar & Catherine
2. Nelly, Joseph, and Zillah, for example
3. ____Dean; housekeeper
4. Word to describe Hareton as a boy
5. He took in Heathcliff
6. Feeling Catherine and Heathcliff have for each other
7. Make tears; boo-hoo
8. Mr. Earnshaw's daughter
9. ____Heights
10. Heathcliff dumps this on Edgar
11. Isabella warns Heathcliff that Hindley has one
12. Isabella's kind of dog
13. Author
14. Catherine threw herself into one and locked herself in her room
15. Hareton hangs a litter of these
16. ____Crags
17. Meeting place for Cathy & Linton
18. Heathcliff's specialty
19. Self-righteous servant of Heathcliff
20. He rented Thrushcross Grange

Wuthering Heights Fill In The Blank 4 Answer Key

CATHY	1.	Daughter of Edgar & Catherine
SERVANTS	2.	Nelly, Joseph, and Zillah, for example
NELLY	3.	____Dean; housekeeper
WILD	4.	Word to describe Hareton as a boy
EARNSHAW	5.	He took in Heathcliff
LOVE	6.	Feeling Catherine and Heathcliff have for each other
CRY	7.	Make tears; boo-hoo
CATHERINE	8.	Mr. Earnshaw's daughter
WUTHERING	9.	____Heights
APPLESAUCE	10.	Heathcliff dumps this on Edgar
GUN	11.	Isabella warns Heathcliff that Hindley has one
SPANIEL	12.	Isabella's kind of dog
BRONTE	13.	Author
FIT	14.	Catherine threw herself into one and locked herself in her room
PUPPIES	15.	Hareton hangs a litter of these
PENISTON	16.	____Crags
MOOR	17.	Meeting place for Cathy & Linton
REVENGE	18.	Heathcliff's specialty
JOSEPH	19.	Self-righteous servant of Heathcliff
LOCKWOOD	20.	He rented Thrushcross Grange

Wuthering Heights Matching 1

___ 1. THRUSHCROSS   A. Cathy's feelings for Linton
___ 2. KIDNAP   B. Meeting place for Cathy & Linton
___ 3. FIT   C. Lockwood's reason for renting Thrushcross Grange
___ 4. SOLITUDE   D. Heathcliff dumps this on Edgar
___ 5. JOSEPH   E. Isabella or Edgar
___ 6. GATE   F. Catherine's brother
___ 7. WILD   G. ____Grange; Linton home estate
___ 8. HEATHCLIFF   H. What Heathcliff wants for Cathy & Linton
___ 9. REVENGE   I. Fence door
___ 10. CARDS   J. What Heathlciff did to Cathy and Nelly
___ 11. MOOR   K. ____Dean; housekeeper
___ 12. HEIR   L. Heathcliff's specialty
___ 13. COUSIN   M. Heathcliff's wife
___ 14. LINTON   N. Word to describe Hareton as a boy
___ 15. PUPPIES   O. Son of Hindley
___ 16. SERVANTS   P. Relationship of Cathy to Linton or Hareton
___ 17. NELLY   Q. Hareton hangs a litter of these
___ 18. HARETON   R. Revenge and Catherine are his passions
___ 19. ISABELLA   S. Gambling game Heathcliff and Hareton played
___ 20. WUTHERING   T. Self-righteous servant of Heathcliff
___ 21. PITY   U. One who inherits
___ 22. APPLESAUCE   V. ____Heights
___ 23. HINDLEY   W. Heathcliff pleads for Catherine's to haunt him
___ 24. MARRIAGE   X. Catherine threw herself into one and locked herself in her room
___ 25. GHOST   Y. Nelly, Joseph, and Zillah, for example

Wuthering Heights Matching 1 Answer Key

G - 1. THRUSHCROSS   A. Cathy's feelings for Linton
J - 2. KIDNAP   B. Meeting place for Cathy & Linton
X - 3. FIT   C. Lockwood's reason for renting Thrushcross Grange
C - 4. SOLITUDE   D. Heathcliff dumps this on Edgar
T - 5. JOSEPH   E. Isabella or Edgar
I - 6. GATE   F. Catherine's brother
N - 7. WILD   G. ____Grange; Linton home estate
R - 8. HEATHCLIFF   H. What Heathcliff wants for Cathy & Linton
L - 9. REVENGE   I. Fence door
S - 10. CARDS   J. What Heathlciff did to Cathy and Nelly
B - 11. MOOR   K. ____Dean; housekeeper
U - 12. HEIR   L. Heathcliff's specialty
P - 13. COUSIN   M. Heathcliff's wife
E - 14. LINTON   N. Word to describe Hareton as a boy
Q - 15. PUPPIES   O. Son of Hindley
Y - 16. SERVANTS   P. Relationship of Cathy to Linton or Hareton
K - 17. NELLY   Q. Hareton hangs a litter of these
O - 18. HARETON   R. Revenge and Catherine are his passions
M - 19. ISABELLA   S. Gambling game Heathcliff and Hareton played
V - 20. WUTHERING   T. Self-righteous servant of Heathcliff
A - 21. PITY   U. One who inherits
D - 22. APPLESAUCE   V. ____Heights
F - 23. HINDLEY   W. Heathcliff pleads for Catherine's to haunt him
H - 24. MARRIAGE   X. Catherine threw herself into one and locked herself in her room
W - 25. GHOST   Y. Nelly, Joseph, and Zillah, for example

Wuthering Heights Matching 2

___ 1. NELLY   A. Fence door
___ 2. SICKLY   B. ____Dean; housekeeper
___ 3. LETTERS   C. Relationship of Cathy to Linton or Hareton
___ 4. HARETON   D. Hindley's wife
___ 5. ISABELLA   E. One who inherits
___ 6. EARNSHAW   F. Describes Linton
___ 7. COUSIN   G. Nelly cuts these off between Cathy and Linton
___ 8. WUTHERING   H. Revenge and Catherine are his passions
___ 9. CATHY   I. Son of Hindley
___10. ZILLAH   J. Make tears; boo-hoo
___11. GATE   K. What Heathcliff wants for Cathy & Linton
___12. JOSEPH   L. Heathcliff holds these on Wuthering Heights
___13. HEIR   M. ____Heights
___14. HINDLEY   N. Mr. Earnshaw's daughter
___15. GUN   O. Hareton hangs a litter of these
___16. GHOST   P. Self-righteous servant of Heathcliff
___17. CATHERINE   Q. Heathcliff's wife
___18. MORTGAGES   R. He took in Heathcliff
___19. PUPPIES   S. ____Crags
___20. MARRIAGE   T. Replaced Nelly at Wuthering Heights
___21. CRY   U. Catherine's brother
___22. WILD   V. Word to describe Hareton as a boy
___23. HEATHCLIFF   W. Daughter of Edgar & Catherine
___24. PENISTON   X. Heathcliff pleads for Catherine's to haunt him
___25. FRANCES   Y. Isabella warns Heathcliff that Hindley has one

Wuthering Heights Matching 2 Answer Key

B - 1. NELLY	A. Fence door
F - 2. SICKLY	B. ____Dean; housekeeper
G - 3. LETTERS	C. Relationship of Cathy to Linton or Hareton
I - 4. HARETON	D. Hindley's wife
Q - 5. ISABELLA	E. One who inherits
R - 6. EARNSHAW	F. Describes Linton
C - 7. COUSIN	G. Nelly cuts these off between Cathy and Linton
M - 8. WUTHERING	H. Revenge and Catherine are his passions
W - 9. CATHY	I. Son of Hindley
T - 10. ZILLAH	J. Make tears; boo-hoo
A - 11. GATE	K. What Heathcliff wants for Cathy & Linton
P - 12. JOSEPH	L. Heathcliff holds these on Wuthering Heights
E - 13. HEIR	M. ____Heights
U - 14. HINDLEY	N. Mr. Earnshaw's daughter
Y - 15. GUN	O. Hareton hangs a litter of these
X - 16. GHOST	P. Self-righteous servant of Heathcliff
N - 17. CATHERINE	Q. Heathcliff's wife
L - 18. MORTGAGES	R. He took in Heathcliff
O - 19. PUPPIES	S. ____Crags
K - 20. MARRIAGE	T. Replaced Nelly at Wuthering Heights
J - 21. CRY	U. Catherine's brother
V - 22. WILD	V. Word to describe Hareton as a boy
H - 23. HEATHCLIFF	W. Daughter of Edgar & Catherine
S - 24. PENISTON	X. Heathcliff pleads for Catherine's to haunt him
D - 25. FRANCES	Y. Isabella warns Heathcliff that Hindley has one

Wuthering Heights Matching 3

___ 1. BRONTE   A. ____Grange; Linton home estate
___ 2. SICKLY   B. Meeting place for Cathy & Linton
___ 3. MOOR   C. Son of Hindley
___ 4. WUTHERING   D. He took in Heathcliff
___ 5. THRUSHCROSS   E. Final resting place
___ 6. FRANCES   F. Lockwood's reason for renting Thrushcross Grange
___ 7. NELLY   G. Author
___ 8. MORTGAGES   H. Daughter of Edgar & Catherine
___ 9. CATHY   I. Hindley's wife
___10. SERVANTS   J. Heathcliff holds these on Wuthering Heights
___11. PENISTON   K. Describes Linton
___12. COUSIN   L. Feeling Catherine and Heathcliff have for each other
___13. SOLITUDE   M. Heathcliff's specialty
___14. EARNSHAW   N. Heathcliff pleads for Catherine's to haunt him
___15. LOVE   O. Isabella warns Heathcliff that Hindley has one
___16. LETTERS   P. ____Crags
___17. ZILLAH   Q. Nelly, Joseph, and Zillah, for example
___18. GHOST   R. ____Dean; housekeeper
___19. LOCK   S. Catherine ___ed her door & stayed in her room
___20. DREAM   T. Catherine appears to Lockwood in a ____
___21. REVENGE   U. Replaced Nelly at Wuthering Heights
___22. GUN   V. Relationship of Cathy to Linton or Hareton
___23. APPLESAUCE   W. Heathcliff dumps this on Edgar
___24. GRAVE   X. ____Heights
___25. HARETON   Y. Nelly cuts these off between Cathy and Linton

Wuthering Heights Matching 3 Answer Key

G - 1. BRONTE	A.	____Grange; Linton home estate
K - 2. SICKLY	B.	Meeting place for Cathy & Linton
B - 3. MOOR	C.	Son of Hindley
X - 4. WUTHERING	D.	He took in Heathcliff
A - 5. THRUSHCROSS	E.	Final resting place
I - 6. FRANCES	F.	Lockwood's reason for renting Thrushcross Grange
R - 7. NELLY	G.	Author
J - 8. MORTGAGES	H.	Daughter of Edgar & Catherine
H - 9. CATHY	I.	Hindley's wife
Q -10. SERVANTS	J.	Heathcliff holds these on Wuthering Heights
P -11. PENISTON	K.	Describes Linton
V -12. COUSIN	L.	Feeling Catherine and Heathcliff have for each other
F -13. SOLITUDE	M.	Heathcliff's specialty
D -14. EARNSHAW	N.	Heathcliff pleads for Catherine's to haunt him
L -15. LOVE	O.	Isabella warns Heathcliff that Hindley has one
Y -16. LETTERS	P.	____Crags
U -17. ZILLAH	Q.	Nelly, Joseph, and Zillah, for example
N -18. GHOST	R.	____Dean; housekeeper
S -19. LOCK	S.	Catherine ____ed her door & stayed in her room
T -20. DREAM	T.	Catherine appears to Lockwood in a ____
M -21. REVENGE	U.	Replaced Nelly at Wuthering Heights
O -22. GUN	V.	Relationship of Cathy to Linton or Hareton
W -23. APPLESAUCE	W.	Heathcliff dumps this on Edgar
E -24. GRAVE	X.	____Heights
C -25. HARETON	Y.	Nelly cuts these off between Cathy and Linton

Wuthering Heights Matching 4

___ 1. MORTGAGES   A. Meeting place for Cathy & Linton
___ 2. GATE   B. Lockwood's reason for renting Thrushcross Grange
___ 3. BRONTE   C. Fence door
___ 4. PITY   D. Self-righteous servant of Heathcliff
___ 5. CATHERINE   E. Son of Hindley
___ 6. HARETON   F. Cathy's feelings for Linton
___ 7. SOLITUDE   G. Hindley's wife
___ 8. EDGAR   H. Isabella warns Heathcliff that Hindley has one
___ 9. THRUSHCROSS   I. Catherine ___ed her door & stayed in her room
___ 10. FRANCES   J. One who inherits
___ 11. LOVE   K. Author
___ 12. SICKLY   L. Heathcliff holds these on Wuthering Heights
___ 13. JOSEPH   M. Nelly cuts these off between Cathy and Linton
___ 14. ZILLAH   N. Make tears; boo-hoo
___ 15. COUSIN   O. Heathcliff dumps this on Edgar
___ 16. HEIR   P. Feeling Catherine and Heathcliff have for each other
___ 17. APPLESAUCE   Q. Replaced Nelly at Wuthering Heights
___ 18. LETTERS   R. Mr. Earnshaw's daughter
___ 19. MOOR   S. Relationship of Cathy to Linton or Hareton
___ 20. SERVANTS   T. Catherine's Husband
___ 21. GUN   U. Describes Linton
___ 22. LOCK   V. Daughter of Edgar & Catherine
___ 23. CATHY   W. Heathcliff's specialty
___ 24. REVENGE   X. Nelly, Joseph, and Zillah, for example
___ 25. CRY   Y. ____Grange; Linton home estate

Wuthering Heights Matching 4 Answer Key

L - 1. MORTGAGES   A. Meeting place for Cathy & Linton
C - 2. GATE   B. Lockwood's reason for renting Thrushcross Grange
K - 3. BRONTE   C. Fence door
F - 4. PITY   D. Self-righteous servant of Heathcliff
R - 5. CATHERINE   E. Son of Hindley
E - 6. HARETON   F. Cathy's feelings for Linton
B - 7. SOLITUDE   G. Hindley's wife
T - 8. EDGAR   H. Isabella warns Heathcliff that Hindley has one
Y - 9. THRUSHCROSS   I. Catherine ___ed her door & stayed in her room
G -10. FRANCES   J. One who inherits
P -11. LOVE   K. Author
U -12. SICKLY   L. Heathcliff holds these on Wuthering Heights
D -13. JOSEPH   M. Nelly cuts these off between Cathy and Linton
Q -14. ZILLAH   N. Make tears; boo-hoo
S -15. COUSIN   O. Heathcliff dumps this on Edgar
J -16. HEIR   P. Feeling Catherine and Heathcliff have for each other
O -17. APPLESAUCE   Q. Replaced Nelly at Wuthering Heights
M -18. LETTERS   R. Mr. Earnshaw's daughter
A -19. MOOR   S. Relationship of Cathy to Linton or Hareton
X -20. SERVANTS   T. Catherine's Husband
H -21. GUN   U. Describes Linton
I -22. LOCK   V. Daughter of Edgar & Catherine
V -23. CATHY   W. Heathcliff's specialty
W -24. REVENGE   X. Nelly, Joseph, and Zillah, for example
N -25. CRY   Y. ___Grange; Linton home estate

Wuthering Heights Magic Squares 1

A. WUTHERING
B. EARNSHAW
C. HARETON
D. PUPPIES
E. LOCKWOOD
F. JOSEPH
G. FRANCES
H. PENISTON
I. BRONTE
J. CATHY
K. ZILLAH
L. SPANIEL
M. REVENGE
N. MORTGAGES
O. SICKLY
P. CARDS

1. ____Crags
2. Heathcliff's specialty
3. He took in Heathcliff
4. Replaced Nelly at Wuthering Heights
5. Daughter of Edgar & Catherine
6. Son of Hindley
7. Gambling game Heathcliff and Hareton played
8. He rented Thrushcross Grange
9. Describes Linton
10. Self-righteous servant of Heathcliff
11. Author
12. Hareton hangs a litter of these
13. ____Heights
14. Isabella's kind of dog
15. Hindley's wife
16. Heathcliff holds these on Wuthering Heights

A=	B=	C=	D=
E=	F=	G=	H=
I=	J=	K=	L=
M=	N=	O=	P=

Wuthering Heights Magic Squares 1 Answer Key

A. WUTHERING
B. EARNSHAW
C. HARETON
D. PUPPIES
E. LOCKWOOD
F. JOSEPH
G. FRANCES
H. PENISTON
I. BRONTE
J. CATHY
K. ZILLAH
L. SPANIEL
M. REVENGE
N. MORTGAGES
O. SICKLY
P. CARDS

1. ____Crags
2. Heathcliff's specialty
3. He took in Heathcliff
4. Replaced Nelly at Wuthering Heights
5. Daughter of Edgar & Catherine
6. Son of Hindley
7. Gambling game Heathcliff and Hareton played
8. He rented Thrushcross Grange
9. Describes Linton
10. Self-righteous servant of Heathcliff
11. Author
12. Hareton hangs a litter of these
13. ____Heights
14. Isabella's kind of dog
15. Hindley's wife
16. Heathcliff holds these on Wuthering Heights

A=13	B=3	C=6	D=12
E=8	F=10	G=15	H=1
I=11	J=5	K=4	L=14
M=2	N=16	O=9	P=7

Wuthering Heights Magic Squares 2

A. CRY
B. APPLESAUCE
C. MORTGAGES
D. CATHY
E. GRAVE
F. LETTERS
G. MOOR
H. HINDLEY
I. SICKLY
J. THRUSHCROSS
K. PUPPIES
L. LINTON
M. REVENGE
N. SPANIEL
O. PENISTON
P. LOVE

1. Catherine's brother
2. Heathcliff's specialty
3. Heathcliff dumps this on Edgar
4. Hareton hangs a litter of these
5. ____Grange; Linton home estate
6. Heathcliff holds these on Wuthering Heights
7. Feeling Catherine and Heathcliff have for each other
8. Final resting place
9. ____Crags
10. Nelly cuts these off between Cathy and Linton
11. Describes Linton
12. Daughter of Edgar & Catherine
13. Make tears; boo-hoo
14. Isabella or Edgar
15. Meeting place for Cathy & Linton
16. Isabella's kind of dog

A=	B=	C=	D=
E=	F=	G=	H=
I=	J=	K=	L=
M=	N=	O=	P=

Wuthering Heights Magic Squares 2 Answer Key

A. CRY
B. APPLESAUCE
C. MORTGAGES
D. CATHY
E. GRAVE
F. LETTERS
G. MOOR
H. HINDLEY
I. SICKLY
J. THRUSHCROSS
K. PUPPIES
L. LINTON
M. REVENGE
N. SPANIEL
O. PENISTON
P. LOVE

1. Catherine's brother
2. Heathcliff's specialty
3. Heathcliff dumps this on Edgar
4. Hareton hangs a litter of these
5. ____Grange; Linton home estate
6. Heathcliff holds these on Wuthering Heights
7. Feeling Catherine and Heathcliff have for each other
8. Final resting place
9. ____Crags
10. Nelly cuts these off between Cathy and Linton
11. Describes Linton
12. Daughter of Edgar & Catherine
13. Make tears; boo-hoo
14. Isabella or Edgar
15. Meeting place for Cathy & Linton
16. Isabella's kind of dog

A=13	B=3	C=6	D=12
E=8	F=10	G=15	H=1
I=11	J=5	K=4	L=14
M=2	N=16	O=9	P=7

Wuthering Heights Magic Squares 3

A. PUPPIES
B. JOSEPH
C. WUTHERING
D. CATHY
E. FIT
F. MORTGAGES
G. CATHERINE
H. GUN
I. ZILLAH
J. SERVANTS
K. GATE
L. MARRIAGE
M. SOLITUDE
N. HEATHCLIFF
O. GRAVE
P. PITY

1. Hareton hangs a litter of these
2. Revenge and Catherine are his passions
3. Nelly, Joseph, and Zillah, for example
4. Catherine threw herself into one and locked herself in her room
5. Mr. Earnshaw's daughter
6. What Heathcliff wants for Cathy & Linton
7. Cathy's feelings for Linton
8. ____ Heights
9. Final resting place
10. Daughter of Edgar & Catherine
11. Isabella warns Heathcliff that Hindley has one
12. Fence door
13. Replaced Nelly at Wuthering Heights
14. Heathcliff holds these on Wuthering Heights
15. Self-righteous servant of Heathcliff
16. Lockwood's reason for renting Thrushcross Grange

A=	B=	C=	D=
E=	F=	G=	H=
I=	J=	K=	L=
M=	N=	O=	P=

Wuthering Heights Magic Squares 3 Answer Key

A. PUPPIES
B. JOSEPH
C. WUTHERING
D. CATHY
E. FIT
F. MORTGAGES
G. CATHERINE
H. GUN
I. ZILLAH
J. SERVANTS
K. GATE
L. MARRIAGE
M. SOLITUDE
N. HEATHCLIFF
O. GRAVE
P. PITY

1. Hareton hangs a litter of these
2. Revenge and Catherine are his passions
3. Nelly, Joseph, and Zillah, for example
4. Catherine threw herself into one and locked herself in her room
5. Mr. Earnshaw's daughter
6. What Heathcliff wants for Cathy & Linton
7. Cathy's feelings for Linton
8. ____Heights
9. Final resting place
10. Daughter of Edgar & Catherine
11. Isabella warns Heathcliff that Hindley has one
12. Fence door
13. Replaced Nelly at Wuthering Heights
14. Heathcliff holds these on Wuthering Heights
15. Self-righteous servant of Heathcliff
16. Lockwood's reason for renting Thrushcross Grange

A=1	B=15	C=8	D=10
E=4	F=14	G=5	H=11
I=13	J=3	K=12	L=6
M=16	N=2	O=9	P=7

Wuthering Heights Magic Squares 4

A. KIDNAP
B. LOCK
C. FRANCES
D. GATE
E. PUPPIES
F. GRAVE
G. LOVE
H. HEIR
I. LINTON
J. CATHY
K. CATHERINE
L. EARNSHAW
M. WUTHERING
N. MARRIAGE
O. PITY
P. CARDS

1. Cathy's feelings for Linton
2. Daughter of Edgar & Catherine
3. One who inherits
4. What Heathlciff did to Cathy and Nelly
5. Fence door
6. Hareton hangs a litter of these
7. Mr. Earnshaw's daughter
8. What Heathcliff wants for Cathy & Linton
9. Final resting place
10. Hindley's wife
11. ____Heights
12. He took in Heathcliff
13. Isabella or Edgar
14. Gambling game Heathcliff and Hareton played
15. Catherine ___ed her door & stayed in her room
16. Feeling Catherine and Heathcliff have for each other

A=	B=	C=	D=
E=	F=	G=	H=
I=	J=	K=	L=
M=	N=	O=	P=

27 Copyright 2005 Teacher's Pet Publications

Wuthering Heights Magic Squares 4 Answer Key

A. KIDNAP
B. LOCK
C. FRANCES
D. GATE
E. PUPPIES
F. GRAVE
G. LOVE
H. HEIR
I. LINTON
J. CATHY
K. CATHERINE
L. EARNSHAW
M. WUTHERING
N. MARRIAGE
O. PITY
P. CARDS

1. Cathy's feelings for Linton
2. Daughter of Edgar & Catherine
3. One who inherits
4. What Heathlciff did to Cathy and Nelly
5. Fence door
6. Hareton hangs a litter of these
7. Mr. Earnshaw's daughter
8. What Heathcliff wants for Cathy & Linton
9. Final resting place
10. Hindley's wife
11. ____Heights
12. He took in Heathcliff
13. Isabella or Edgar
14. Gambling game Heathcliff and Hareton played
15. Catherine ___ed her door & stayed in her room
16. Feeling Catherine and Heathcliff have for each other

A=4	B=15	C=10	D=5
E=6	F=9	G=16	H=3
I=13	J=2	K=7	L=12
M=11	N=8	O=1	P=14

Wuthering Heights Word Search 1

```
W W V T H R U S H C R O S S D R A C
U K I D N A P E I K R Y N E C J P T
T F F L H N I S C D Y Y G R H P C
H P N T D I N P V D K E D A B A L P
E I T X S L R P Z M D L M G H R E D
R T S U B E S U R N R D Y T L E S C
I Y O A K T R P G D E N M R O T A D
N C X N B T B V R P A I O O C O U T
G J G A T E Z Q A E M H O M K N C X
T M O Z B R L W V N V N R C W X E Z
V H M S Y S X L E I T E T W O L T C
G P P M E R T D A S F S N G O P N J
E D G A R P U Y K T S O H G D Y O P
Y B V N K T H C Y O W V K W E L R Y
P K D L I T O L R N R Y G L F O B L
Q N S L A L L Z I L L A H U B V J D
M N O C X E N C A T H E R I N E G K
Y S P A N I E L I N T O N H E I R W
```

Author (6)
Catherine ___ed her door & stayed in her room (4)
Catherine appears to Lockwood in a ____ (5)
Catherine threw herself into one and locked herself in her room (3)
Catherine's Husband (5)
Catherine's brother (7)
Cathy's feelings for Linton (4)
Daughter of Edgar & Catherine (5)
Describes Linton (6)
Feeling Catherine and Heathcliff have for each other (4)
Fence door (4)
Final resting place (5)
Gambling game Heathcliff and Hareton played (5)
Hareton hangs a litter of these (7)
He rented Thrushcross Grange (8)
Heathcliff dumps this on Edgar (10)
Heathcliff holds these on Wuthering Heights (9)
Heathcliff pleads for Catherine's to haunt him (5)
Heathcliff's specialty (7)
Heathcliff's wife (8)
Isabella or Edgar (6)
Isabella warns Heathcliff that Hindley has one (3)
Isabella's kind of dog (7)
Lockwood's reason for renting Thrushcross Grange (8)
Make tears; boo-hoo (3)
Meeting place for Cathy & Linton (4)
Mr. Earnshaw's daughter (9)
Nelly cuts these off between Cathy and Linton (7)
Nelly, Joseph, and Zillah, for example (8)
One who inherits (4)
Relationship of Cathy to Linton or Hareton (6)
Replaced Nelly at Wuthering Heights (6)
Self-righteous servant of Heathcliff (6)
Son of Hindley (7)
What Heathlciff did to Cathy and Nelly (6)
Word to describe Hareton as a boy (4)
____Crags (8)
____Dean; housekeeper (5)
____Grange; Linton home estate (11)
____Heights (9)

Wuthering Heights Word Search 1 Answer Key

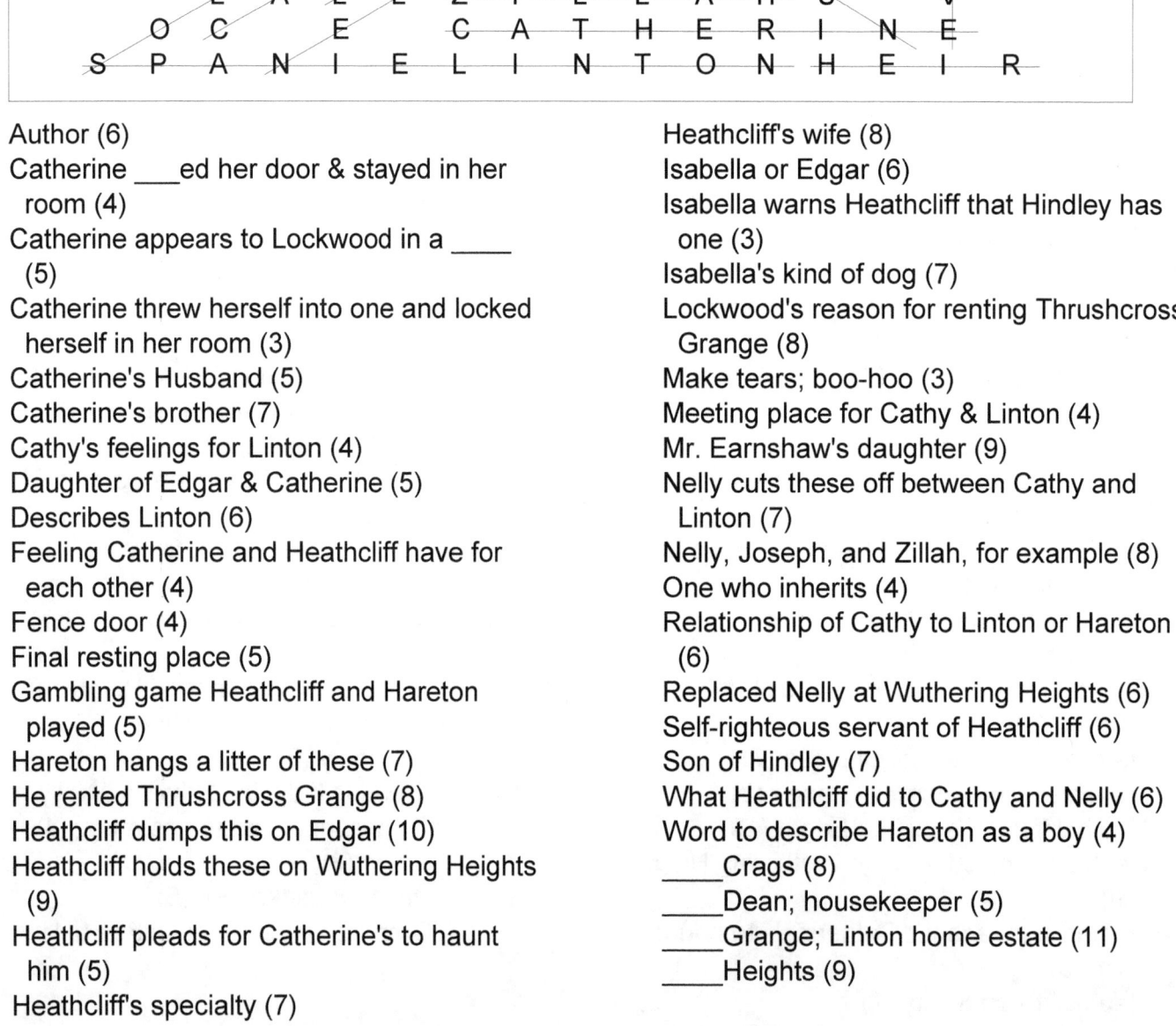

Author (6)
Catherine ___ed her door & stayed in her room (4)
Catherine appears to Lockwood in a ____ (5)
Catherine threw herself into one and locked herself in her room (3)
Catherine's Husband (5)
Catherine's brother (7)
Cathy's feelings for Linton (4)
Daughter of Edgar & Catherine (5)
Describes Linton (6)
Feeling Catherine and Heathcliff have for each other (4)
Fence door (4)
Final resting place (5)
Gambling game Heathcliff and Hareton played (5)
Hareton hangs a litter of these (7)
He rented Thrushcross Grange (8)
Heathcliff dumps this on Edgar (10)
Heathcliff holds these on Wuthering Heights (9)
Heathcliff pleads for Catherine's to haunt him (5)
Heathcliff's specialty (7)

Heathcliff's wife (8)
Isabella or Edgar (6)
Isabella warns Heathcliff that Hindley has one (3)
Isabella's kind of dog (7)
Lockwood's reason for renting Thrushcross Grange (8)
Make tears; boo-hoo (3)
Meeting place for Cathy & Linton (4)
Mr. Earnshaw's daughter (9)
Nelly cuts these off between Cathy and Linton (7)
Nelly, Joseph, and Zillah, for example (8)
One who inherits (4)
Relationship of Cathy to Linton or Hareton (6)
Replaced Nelly at Wuthering Heights (6)
Self-righteous servant of Heathcliff (6)
Son of Hindley (7)
What Heathlciff did to Cathy and Nelly (6)
Word to describe Hareton as a boy (4)
____Crags (8)
____Dean; housekeeper (5)
____Grange; Linton home estate (11)
____Heights (9)

Wuthering Heights Word Search 2

```
L R E V E N G E M O O R Z H S P N D
O E C U A S E L P P A J I E Y E B W
C N T K X X R H U F V R L A H N B J
K C X P Q G C I P Z W C L T D I N T
W P D Y G B Q N P F N A A H C S N H
O H H W F A E D I I P T H C A T K G
O T C H T V T L E D T H L R O U M
D S H R A G D E S C R Y K I D N A P
L F P R S A Y C N S E S F S P J F
I I G A U R E P W V B A A F Y T O N
N T X Y N S G T G U B R L M B F S X
T J Y S I I H D O E T P O L D T E K
O Y H Z S C E C L N C H V N N P P Q
N A R Z U K V L R G L T E A T Y H V
W T X C O L A J I O S O V R L E T Q
R L P B C Y Y P E O S R C L I D L D
M A R R I A G E H W E S E K C N T B
J M O R T G A G E S B N W I L D G N
```

Author (6)
Catherine ___ed her door & stayed in her room (4)
Catherine appears to Lockwood in a ____ (5)
Catherine threw herself into one and locked herself in her room (3)
Catherine's Husband (5)
Catherine's brother (7)
Cathy's feelings for Linton (4)
Daughter of Edgar & Catherine (5)
Describes Linton (6)
Feeling Catherine and Heathcliff have for each other (4)
Fence door (4)
Final resting place (5)
Gambling game Heathcliff and Hareton played (5)
Hareton hangs a litter of these (7)
He rented Thrushcross Grange (8)
He took in Heathcliff (8)
Heathcliff dumps this on Edgar (10)
Heathcliff holds these on Wuthering Heights (9)
Heathcliff pleads for Catherine's to haunt him (5)

Heathcliff's specialty (7)
Heathcliff's wife (8)
Isabella or Edgar (6)
Isabella warns Heathcliff that Hindley has one (3)
Isabella's kind of dog (7)
Make tears; boo-hoo (3)
Meeting place for Cathy & Linton (4)
Nelly, Joseph, and Zillah, for example (8)
One who inherits (4)
Relationship of Cathy to Linton or Hareton (6)
Replaced Nelly at Wuthering Heights (6)
Revenge and Catherine are his passions (10)
Self-righteous servant of Heathcliff (6)
Son of Hindley (7)
What Heathcliff wants for Cathy & Linton (8)
What Heathlciff did to Cathy and Nelly (6)
Word to describe Hareton as a boy (4)
____Crags (8)
____Dean; housekeeper (5)
____Grange; Linton home estate (11)
____Heights (9)

Wuthering Heights Word Search 2 Answer Key

```
L   R  E  V  E  N  G  E  M  O  O  R    Z  H        P
O   E  C  U  A  S  E  L  P  P  A       I  E        E
C                     H  U              L  A        N
K                     I  P           C  L  T        I
W            G        N  P           A  A  H  C     S
O         A  E  D  I  I              T  H  C  A        G
O   T  H  V  T  L  E  D  T        H        L  R  O  U
D   S  R  A  G  D  E  S  C  R  Y  K  I     D  N  A  P
L   F  P  R  R  A  Y              E  S  F  S        J
I   I  G  A  U  R  E     W     B  A  A  F           O
N   T    N  S     T     U  B  R  L  M              S
T         S  I  H     O  E  T     O           T     E
O         H  S  C  E  C  L  N     H  V  N  N        P
N   A        U  K     L  R     L  T  E  A  T  Y  H
W            O  L  A     I  O  S  O  V  R  L  E
             C  Y        E  O  S  R  C  L  I
M   A  R  R  I  A  G  E  H     E  S  E  K     N
    M  O  R  T  G  A  G  E  S     N  W  I  L  D  G
```

Author (6)
Catherine ___ed her door & stayed in her room (4)
Catherine appears to Lockwood in a ____ (5)
Catherine threw herself into one and locked herself in her room (3)
Catherine's Husband (5)
Catherine's brother (7)
Cathy's feelings for Linton (4)
Daughter of Edgar & Catherine (5)
Describes Linton (6)
Feeling Catherine and Heathcliff have for each other (4)
Fence door (4)
Final resting place (5)
Gambling game Heathcliff and Hareton played (5)
Hareton hangs a litter of these (7)
He rented Thrushcross Grange (8)
He took in Heathcliff (8)
Heathcliff dumps this on Edgar (10)
Heathcliff holds these on Wuthering Heights (9)
Heathcliff pleads for Catherine's to haunt him (5)

Heathcliff's specialty (7)
Heathcliff's wife (8)
Isabella or Edgar (6)
Isabella warns Heathcliff that Hindley has one (3)
Isabella's kind of dog (7)
Make tears; boo-hoo (3)
Meeting place for Cathy & Linton (4)
Nelly, Joseph, and Zillah, for example (8)
One who inherits (4)
Relationship of Cathy to Linton or Hareton (6)
Replaced Nelly at Wuthering Heights (6)
Revenge and Catherine are his passions (10)
Self-righteous servant of Heathcliff (6)
Son of Hindley (7)
What Heathcliff wants for Cathy & Linton (8)
What Heathlciff did to Cathy and Nelly (6)
Word to describe Hareton as a boy (4)
____Crags (8)
____Dean; housekeeper (5)
____Grange; Linton home estate (11)
____Heights (9)

Wuthering Heights Word Search 3

```
W U T H E R I N G T T P M A R R I A G E
Z M L A S F E E H K H E F D K E D Y Z F R
S O O L N F C L G J R N R M V A V Z P P
F R C L Y H U L K M U I A K L R D Y S X
G T K I S C A Y W S S N B Z N G H G T
Q G W Z K M S R X S H T C S P S H Q L F
M A O L Q H E V E P C O E E J H S T F Z
T G O E Q G L H U T R N S R Z A D I H Y
Z E D T D G P P L L O C D V K W L Y M Q
C S B T T V P R Z E S N D A N C H D K E
K O L E K I A N F I S R P N H V K Q D W
H C U R E H R F C N E S C T S L D U C R
Y I I S A B E L L A Y G A S F I T P A M
R E N M I T V D M P R E U M S I A J T Z
H E E D A N O L G S H D O N L N Y O H F
D R V G L Q L I I A L O S O D L H S E M
X R A E H E R W K N R L S I K O T E R X
B S R B N O Y G M N T C K C Y C A P I L
Z Z G Q V G S C R Y D O I L Z K C H N T
B R O N T E E T B B X S N P I T Y X E D
```

APPLESAUCE	GUN	MORTGAGES
BRONTE	HARETON	NELLY
CARDS	HEATHCLIFF	PENISTON
CATHERINE	HEIR	PITY
CATHY	HINDLEY	PUPPIES
COUSIN	ISABELLA	REVENGE
CRY	JOSEPH	SERVANTS
DREAM	KIDNAP	SICKLY
EARNSHAW	LETTERS	SOLITUDE
EDGAR	LINTON	SPANIEL
FIT	LOCK	THRUSHCROSS
FRANCES	LOCKWOOD	WILD
GATE	LOVE	WUTHERING
GHOST	MARRIAGE	ZILLAH
GRAVE	MOOR	

Wuthering Heights Word Search 3 Answer Key

```
W U T H E R I N G       T P M A R R I A G E
  M L A       E   L     H E     E
  O O L       C   L     R N     A
  R C L     H U   Y     U I     R
  T K I     A S   R     S S     N
  G W Z     Y S   R   P H T   S S           F
  A O L       E   E   U C O   E H         F
  G O E       L P U   P R N   R I       I
  E D T       P P T   P O D   V W     L
C S   T       P A L   I N     A C   E
H O   E       I   E   E R     N H   D
  U   R       A   C   S       T U   C
  R I S A B E L L A   G A S F I T P A
  E N I T V D M P R E U M     I A J T
  H E D A N O L G S H D O N   N Y O H
    V G L   L I A   O O S   D L H S E
    A A E   W N R   S I K O   K O R
    R R N     O T   I K C A   C S I
      G G S C R Y   O         K P N
B R O N T E E T     S N P I T Y   E
```

APPLESAUCE   GUN   MORTGAGES
BRONTE   HARETON   NELLY
CARDS   HEATHCLIFF   PENISTON
CATHERINE   HEIR   PITY
CATHY   HINDLEY   PUPPIES
COUSIN   ISABELLA   REVENGE
CRY   JOSEPH   SERVANTS
DREAM   KIDNAP   SICKLY
EARNSHAW   LETTERS   SOLITUDE
EDGAR   LINTON   SPANIEL
FIT   LOCK   THRUSHCROSS
FRANCES   LOCKWOOD   WILD
GATE   LOVE   WUTHERING
GHOST   MARRIAGE   ZILLAH
GRAVE   MOOR

34 Copyright 2005 Teacher's Pet Publications

Wuthering Heights Word Search 4

```
B R O N T E C U A S E L P P A M N L F N
Z H W V I S L T P N E D P N U I V O R H
N G N G F D P L I T M C V S S P Z C A N
N N G A U N J R T R T O H U W R P K N T
L I N T O N E E H P E S O J S E D I C Y
S R P E Z H R T C G C C D R N V R R E X
F E D B T S H A D X S K F I J E E S S S
G H M A G I G L C R V L S L K N A P K M
D T C R N G P L M L N T Q C F G M A R D
P U Y D C G D E X T O F Q A Z E R N Q S
I W L G A T L B M N T H R R T I H I J H
T E W X T G V A F A E T P D J P L E G G
Y F H T H R U S H C R O S S I C K L Y J
C V D O Y P O I E M A R Y T R C S H A B
C L S D V L G V D R H G I Y Z Y B C W H
H T L R I N R P G S V R N A M L C T W M
Q I P T K I D N A P F A S D G L O V E H
W F U Q E D M R R G P V N Q N E H V R Z
L D Q H W A H S N R A E F T P N J B Z S
E M O R T G A G E S N W S F S C G C M S
```

APPLESAUCE	GRAVE	MORTGAGES
BRONTE	GUN	NELLY
CARDS	HARETON	PENISTON
CATHERINE	HEIR	PITY
CATHY	HINDLEY	PUPPIES
COUSIN	ISABELLA	REVENGE
CRY	JOSEPH	SERVANTS
DREAM	KIDNAP	SICKLY
EARNSHAW	LETTERS	SOLITUDE
EDGAR	LINTON	SPANIEL
FIT	LOCK	THRUSHCROSS
FRANCES	LOVE	WILD
GATE	MARRIAGE	WUTHERING
GHOST	MOOR	ZILLAH

Wuthering Heights Word Search 4 Answer Key

APPLESAUCE	GRAVE	MORTGAGES
BRONTE	GUN	NELLY
CARDS	HARETON	PENISTON
CATHERINE	HEIR	PITY
CATHY	HINDLEY	PUPPIES
COUSIN	ISABELLA	REVENGE
CRY	JOSEPH	SERVANTS
DREAM	KIDNAP	SICKLY
EARNSHAW	LETTERS	SOLITUDE
EDGAR	LINTON	SPANIEL
FIT	LOCK	THRUSHCROSS
FRANCES	LOVE	WILD
GATE	MARRIAGE	WUTHERING
GHOST	MOOR	ZILLAH

Wuthering Heights Crossword 1

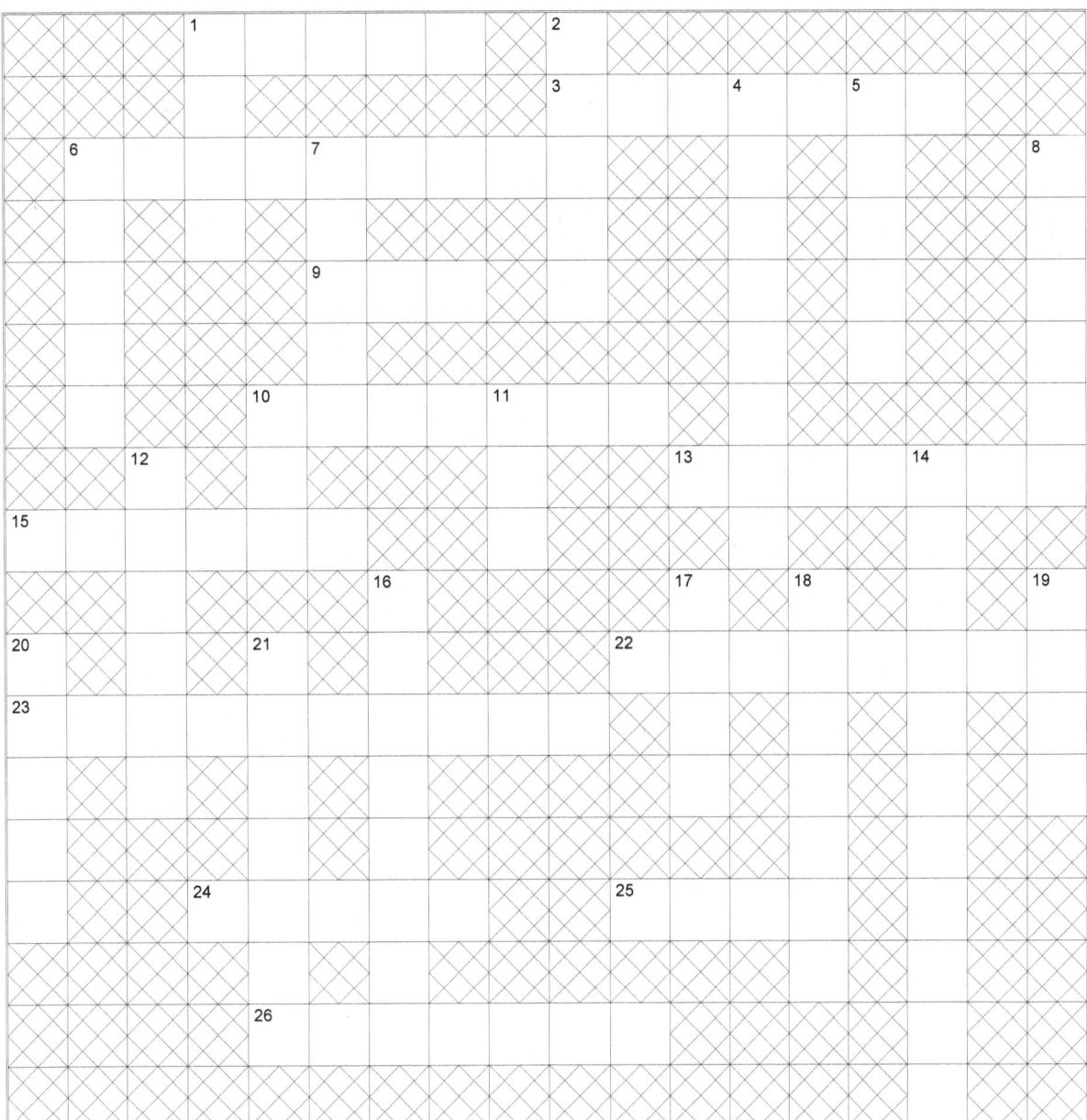

Across
1. Heathcliff pleads for Catherine's to haunt him
3. Heathcliff's specialty
6. Mr. Earnshaw's daughter
9. Isabella warns Heathcliff that Hindley has one
10. Hindley's wife
13. Son of Hindley
15. Author
22. Lockwood's reason for renting Thrushcross Grange
23. Heathcliff dumps this on Edgar
24. ____Dean; housekeeper
25. Feeling Catherine and Heathcliff have for each other
26. Isabella's kind of dog

Down
1. Fence door
2. Catherine appears to Lockwood in a ____
4. He took in Heathcliff
5. Final resting place
6. Daughter of Edgar & Catherine
7. Catherine's Husband
8. Relationship of Cathy to Linton or Hareton
10. Catherine threw herself into one and locked herself in her room
11. Make tears; boo-hoo
12. Self-righteous servant of Heathcliff
14. ____Grange; Linton home estate
16. Heathcliff's wife
17. Catherine ___ed her door & stayed in her room
18. Catherine's brother
19. One who inherits
20. Gambling game Heathcliff and Hareton played
21. Nelly cuts these off between Cathy and Linton

Wuthering Heights Crossword 1 Answer Key

[Crossword grid with the following answers:]

Across:
1. GHOST
3. REVENGE
6. CATHERINE
9. GUN
10. FRANCES
13. HARETON
15. BRONTE
22. SOLITUDE
23. APPLESAUCE
24. NELLY
25. LOVE
26. SPANIEL

Down:
1. GATHY
2. DREAM
4. EARNSHAW
5. GRAVE
6. CATHY
7. EDGAR
8. COUSIN
10. FIRE
11. CRY
12. JOSEPH
14. THRUSHCROSS (THRUSH)
16. ISABELLA
17. LOCKED
18. HINDLEY
19. HEIR
20. CARDS
21. LETTERS

Across
1. Heathcliff pleads for Catherine's to haunt him
3. Heathcliff's specialty
6. Mr. Earnshaw's daughter
9. Isabella warns Heathcliff that Hindley has one
10. Hindley's wife
13. Son of Hindley
15. Author
22. Lockwood's reason for renting Thrushcross Grange
23. Heathcliff dumps this on Edgar
24. ____Dean; housekeeper
25. Feeling Catherine and Heathcliff have for each other
26. Isabella's kind of dog

Down
1. Fence door
2. Catherine appears to Lockwood in a ____
4. He took in Heathcliff
5. Final resting place
6. Daughter of Edgar & Catherine
7. Catherine's Husband
8. Relationship of Cathy to Linton or Hareton
10. Catherine threw herself into one and locked herself in her room
11. Make tears; boo-hoo
12. Self-righteous servant of Heathcliff
14. ____Grange; Linton home estate
16. Heathcliff's wife
17. Catherine ___ed her door & stayed in her room
18. Catherine's brother
19. One who inherits
20. Gambling game Heathcliff and Hareton played
21. Nelly cuts these off between Cathy and Linton

Wuthering Heights Crossword 2

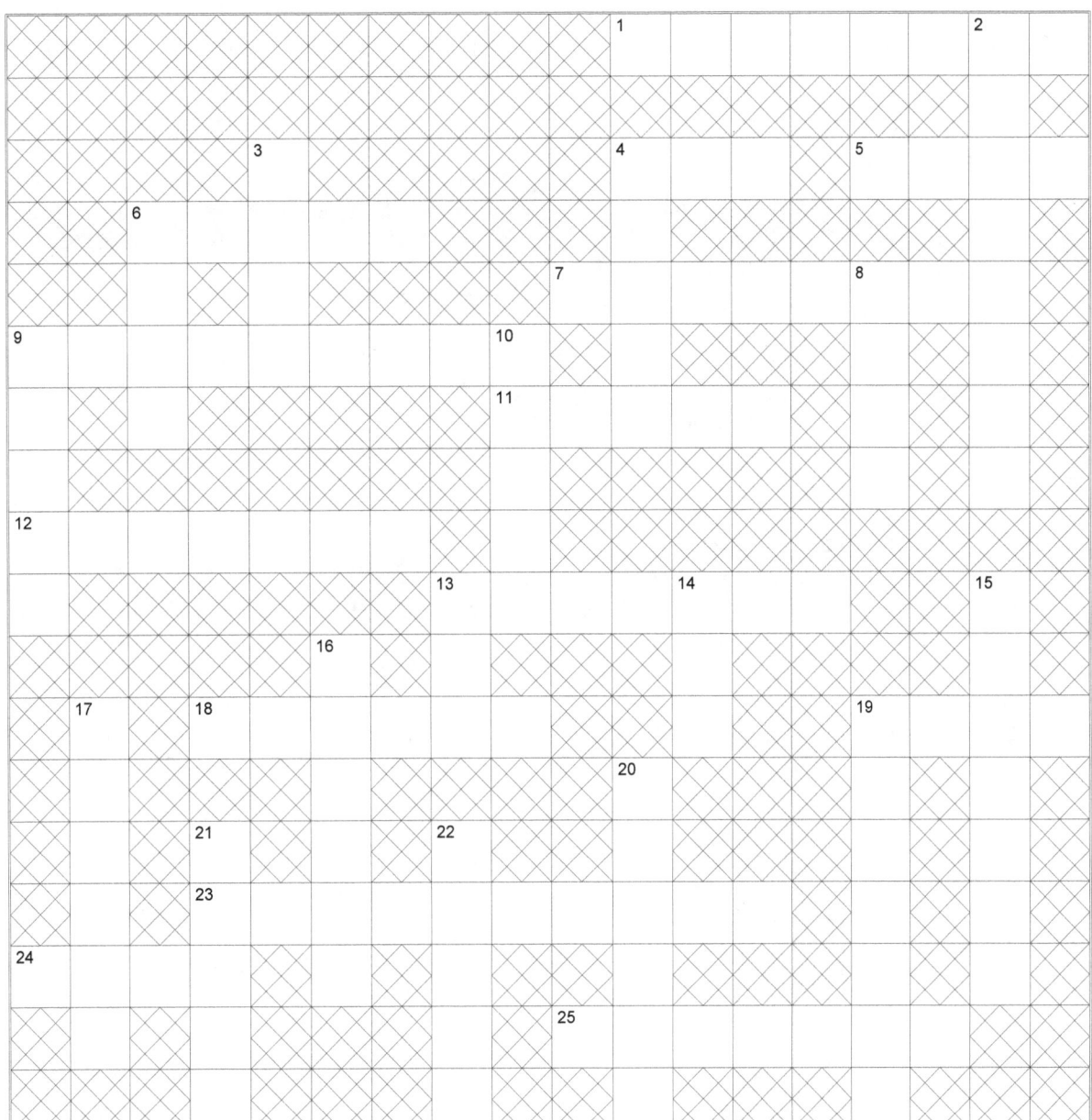

Across
1. Heathcliff's wife
4. Isabella warns Heathcliff that Hindley has one
5. Catherine ___ed her door & stayed in her room
6. Heathcliff pleads for Catherine's to haunt him
7. He took in Heathcliff
9. Mr. Earnshaw's daughter
11. Catherine appears to Lockwood in a ____
12. Son of Hindley
13. Hindley's wife
18. Author
19. Cathy's feelings for Linton
23. Heathcliff dumps this on Edgar
24. Meeting place for Cathy & Linton
25. Catherine's brother

Down
2. He rented Thrushcross Grange
3. Feeling Catherine and Heathcliff have for each other
4. Final resting place
6. Fence door
8. One who inherits
9. Daughter of Edgar & Catherine
10. Catherine's Husband
13. Catherine threw herself into one and locked herself in her room
14. Make tears; boo-hoo
15. Nelly cuts these off between Cathy and Linton
16. Self-righteous servant of Heathcliff
17. Isabella or Edgar
19. Hareton hangs a litter of these
20. Relationship of Cathy to Linton or Hareton
21. Gambling game Heathcliff and Hareton played
22. ____Dean; housekeeper

Wuthering Heights Crossword 2 Answer Key

							¹I	S	A	B	E	L	²L	A
													O	
			³L			⁴G	U	N		⁵L	O	C	K	
		⁶G	H	O	S	T							K	
		A		V			⁷E	A	R	N	S	⁸H	A	W
⁹C	A	T	H	E	R	I	N	¹⁰E				E	O	
A		E						¹¹D	R	E	A	M	O	
T								G				R	D	
¹²H	A	R	E	T	O	N		A						
Y						¹³F	R	A	¹⁴N	C	E	S	¹⁵L	
				¹⁶J		I			R				E	
¹⁷L	¹⁸B	R	O	N	T	E			Y		¹⁹P	I	T	Y
I				S				²⁰C			U		T	
N		²¹C		E		²²N		O			P		E	
T		²³A	P	P	L	E	S	A	U	C	E		R	
²⁴M	O	O	R		H			U			I		S	
N		D					²⁵H	I	N	D	L	E	Y	
S					L		I				S			

Across
1. Heathcliff's wife
4. Isabella warns Heathcliff that Hindley has one
5. Catherine ___ed her door & stayed in her room
6. Heathcliff pleads for Catherine's to haunt him
7. He took in Heathcliff
9. Mr. Earnshaw's daughter
11. Catherine appears to Lockwood in a ____
12. Son of Hindley
13. Hindley's wife
18. Author
19. Cathy's feelings for Linton
23. Heathcliff dumps this on Edgar
24. Meeting place for Cathy & Linton
25. Catherine's brother

Down
2. He rented Thrushcross Grange
3. Feeling Catherine and Heathcliff have for each other
4. Final resting place
6. Fence door
8. One who inherits
9. Daughter of Edgar & Catherine
10. Catherine's Husband
13. Catherine threw herself into one and locked herself in her room
14. Make tears; boo-hoo
15. Nelly cuts these off between Cathy and Linton
16. Self-righteous servant of Heathcliff
17. Isabella or Edgar
19. Hareton hangs a litter of these
20. Relationship of Cathy to Linton or Hareton
21. Gambling game Heathcliff and Hareton played
22. ____Dean; housekeeper

Wuthering Heights Crossword 3

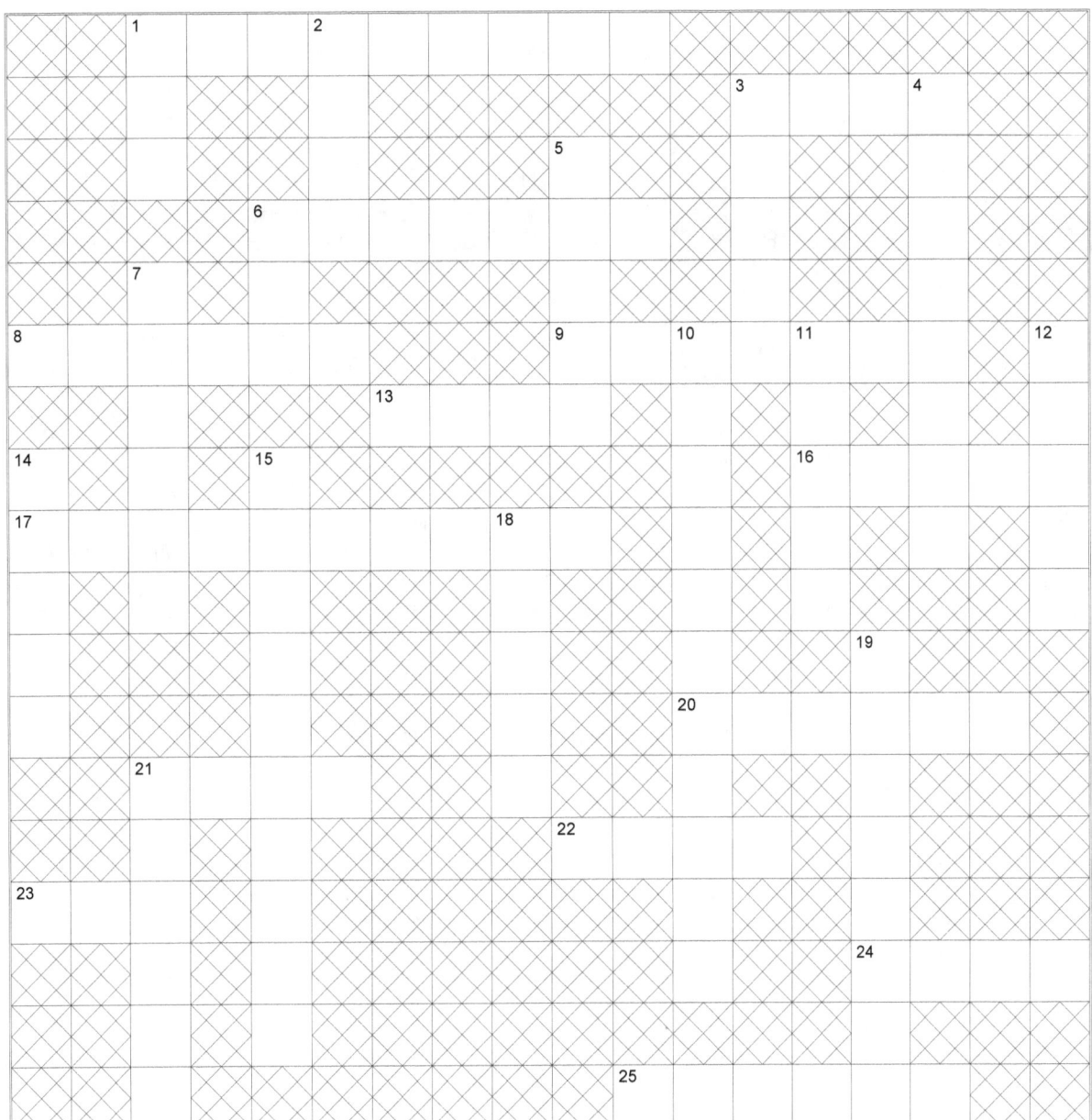

Across
1. Mr. Earnshaw's daughter
3. Fence door
6. Hindley's wife
8. Author
9. Nelly cuts these off between Cathy and Linton
13. Cathy's feelings for Linton
16. Final resting place
17. Heathcliff dumps this on Edgar
20. Relationship of Cathy to Linton or Hareton
21. Catherine ___ed her door & stayed in her room
22. Meeting place for Cathy & Linton
23. Isabella warns Heathcliff that Hindley has one
24. Feeling Catherine and Heathcliff have for each other
25. What Heathlciff did to Cathy and Nelly

Down
1. Make tears; boo-hoo
2. One who inherits
3. Heathcliff pleads for Catherine's to haunt him
4. He took in Heathcliff
5. ____Dean; housekeeper
6. Catherine threw herself into one and locked herself in her room
7. Self-righteous servant of Heathcliff
10. ____Grange; Linton home estate
11. Catherine's Husband
12. Catherine appears to Lockwood in a ____
14. Gambling game Heathcliff and Hareton played
15. Revenge and Catherine are his passions
18. Daughter of Edgar & Catherine
19. Heathcliff's wife
21. Isabella or Edgar

Wuthering Heights Crossword 3 Answer Key

Across
1. Mr. Earnshaw's daughter
3. Fence door
6. Hindley's wife
8. Author
9. Nelly cuts these off between Cathy and Linton
13. Cathy's feelings for Linton
16. Final resting place
17. Heathcliff dumps this on Edgar
20. Relationship of Cathy to Linton or Hareton
21. Catherine ___ed her door & stayed in her room
22. Meeting place for Cathy & Linton
23. Isabella warns Heathcliff that Hindley has one
24. Feeling Catherine and Heathcliff have for each other
25. What Heathlciff did to Cathy and Nelly

Down
1. Make tears; boo-hoo
2. One who inherits
3. Heathcliff pleads for Catherine's to haunt him
4. He took in Heathcliff
5. ___Dean; housekeeper
6. Catherine threw herself into one and locked herself in her room
7. Self-righteous servant of Heathcliff
10. ___Grange; Linton home estate
11. Catherine's Husband
12. Catherine appears to Lockwood in a ___
14. Gambling game Heathcliff and Hareton played
15. Revenge and Catherine are his passions
18. Daughter of Edgar & Catherine
19. Heathcliff's wife
21. Isabella or Edgar

Wuthering Heights Crossword 4

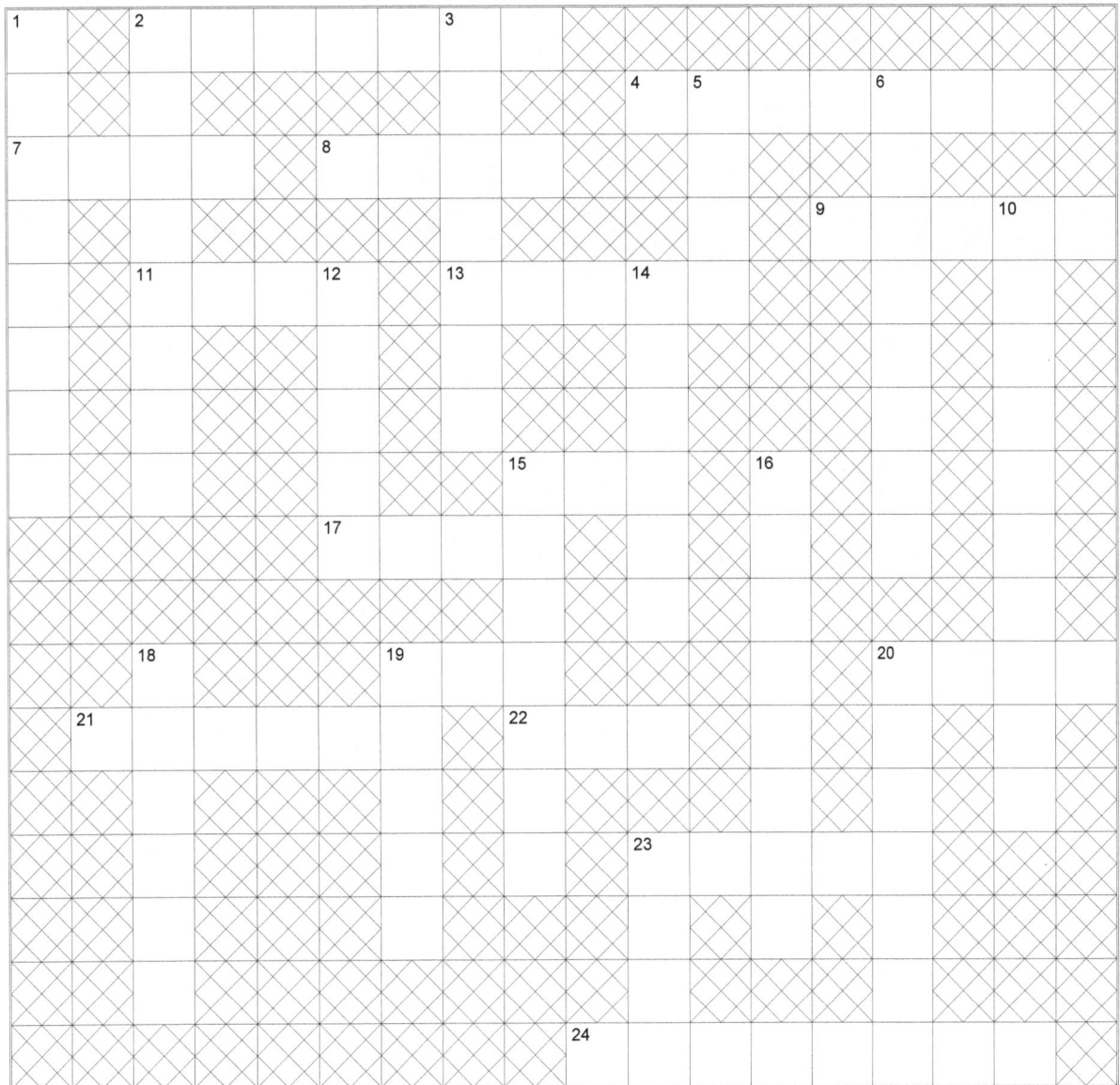

Across
2. Nelly cuts these off between Cathy and Linton
4. Isabella's kind of dog
7. Catherine ___ed her door & stayed in her room
8. Feeling Catherine and Heathcliff have for each other
9. Daughter of Edgar & Catherine
11. Word to describe Hareton as a boy
13. ____Dean; housekeeper
15. Catherine threw herself into one and locked herself in her room
17. Meeting place for Cathy & Linton
19. Isabella warns Heathcliff that Hindley has one
20. One who inherits
21. Replaced Nelly at Wuthering Heights
22. Make tears; boo-hoo
23. Final resting place
24. Nelly, Joseph, and Zillah, for example

Down
1. Lockwood's reason for renting Thrushcross Grange
2. He rented Thrushcross Grange
3. Heathcliff's specialty
5. Cathy's feelings for Linton
6. Heathcliff's wife
10. Revenge and Catherine are his passions
12. Catherine appears to Lockwood in a ____
14. Isabella or Edgar
15. Hindley's wife
16. He took in Heathcliff
18. Describes Linton
19. Heathcliff pleads for Catherine's to haunt him
20. Son of Hindley
23. Fence door

Wuthering Heights Crossword 4 Answer Key

	1 S		2 L	E	T	T	E	R	3 S						
	O		O						E		4 S	5 P	A	N	6 I	E	L
7 L	O	C	K		8 L	O	V	E				I			S	
	I		K				E					T	9 C	A	T	10 H	Y
	T		11 W	I	12 L	D		13 N	E	14 L	L	Y			B		E
	U		O		R			G		I					E		A
	D		O		E			E		N					L		T
	E		D		A			15 F	I	T		16 E			L		H
					17 M	O	O	R		O		A			A		C
								A		N		R					L
			18 S		19 G	U	N					N		20 H	E	I	R
		21 Z	I	L	L	A	H		22 C	R	Y			S		A		F
			C				O		E					H		R		F
			K				S		S		23 G	R	A	V	E		
			L				T				A		W		T		
			Y								T				O		
									24 S	E	R	V	A	N	T	S	

Across
2. Nelly cuts these off between Cathy and Linton
4. Isabella's kind of dog
7. Catherine ___ed her door & stayed in her room
8. Feeling Catherine and Heathcliff have for each other
9. Daughter of Edgar & Catherine
11. Word to describe Hareton as a boy
13. ___Dean; housekeeper
15. Catherine threw herself into one and locked herself in her room
17. Meeting place for Cathy & Linton
19. Isabella warns Heathcliff that Hindley has one
20. One who inherits
21. Replaced Nelly at Wuthering Heights
22. Make tears; boo-hoo
23. Final resting place
24. Nelly, Joseph, and Zillah, for example

Down
1. Lockwood's reason for renting Thrushcross Grange
2. He rented Thrushcross Grange
3. Heathcliff's specialty
5. Cathy's feelings for Linton
6. Heathcliff's wife
10. Revenge and Catherine are his passions
12. Catherine appears to Lockwood in a ____
14. Isabella or Edgar
15. Hindley's wife
16. He took in Heathcliff
18. Describes Linton
19. Heathcliff pleads for Catherine's to haunt him
20. Son of Hindley
23. Fence door

Wuthering Heights

CARDS	COUSIN	MOOR	GUN	KIDNAP
LOCKWOOD	FIT	SOLITUDE	SERVANTS	LINTON
HEIR	LOVE	FREE SPACE	BRONTE	EDGAR
LOCK	NELLY	GHOST	LETTERS	HEATHCLIFF
HARETON	WILD	MORTGAGES	WUTHERING	APPLESAUCE

Wuthering Heights

GRAVE	PITY	EARNSHAW	SPANIEL	MARRIAGE
PENISTON	FRANCES	DREAM	THRUSHCROSS	REVENGE
CATHY	CATHERINE	FREE SPACE	JOSEPH	PUPPIES
HINDLEY	ZILLAH	SICKLY	GATE	APPLESAUCE
WUTHERING	MORTGAGES	WILD	HARETON	HEATHCLIFF

Wuthering Heights

NELLY	GRAVE	FRANCES	LINTON	BRONTE
GUN	PUPPIES	KIDNAP	SICKLY	ISABELLA
EARNSHAW	HEIR	FREE SPACE	REVENGE	ZILLAH
GHOST	SERVANTS	LETTERS	HINDLEY	LOCKWOOD
MORTGAGES	CARDS	LOCK	SPANIEL	EDGAR

Wuthering Heights

DREAM	PENISTON	JOSEPH	WUTHERING	CATHY
COUSIN	MOOR	LOVE	SOLITUDE	MARRIAGE
GATE	THRUSHCROSS	FREE SPACE	CRY	CATHERINE
WILD	HARETON	PITY	FIT	EDGAR
SPANIEL	LOCK	CARDS	MORTGAGES	LOCKWOOD

Wuthering Heights

ZILLAH	PUPPIES	GATE	EARNSHAW	WUTHERING
PENISTON	ISABELLA	NELLY	HEIR	LETTERS
CATHERINE	BRONTE	FREE SPACE	GHOST	SPANIEL
REVENGE	LOCK	GUN	CARDS	SOLITUDE
WILD	MORTGAGES	EDGAR	LINTON	APPLESAUCE

Wuthering Heights

COUSIN	GRAVE	MARRIAGE	LOVE	FIT
SICKLY	JOSEPH	PITY	LOCKWOOD	KIDNAP
CATHY	THRUSHCROSS	FREE SPACE	CRY	FRANCES
SERVANTS	HARETON	HEATHCLIFF	HINDLEY	APPLESAUCE
LINTON	EDGAR	MORTGAGES	WILD	SOLITUDE

Wuthering Heights

LOVE	MARRIAGE	DREAM	JOSEPH	BRONTE
LINTON	NELLY	MOOR	GUN	CATHERINE
FRANCES	PITY	FREE SPACE	GHOST	SPANIEL
EARNSHAW	COUSIN	SICKLY	FIT	SERVANTS
ZILLAH	THRUSHCROSS	HEATHCLIFF	LETTERS	LOCK

Wuthering Heights

HARETON	WILD	LOCKWOOD	GRAVE	PENISTON
SOLITUDE	CATHY	ISABELLA	MORTGAGES	REVENGE
EDGAR	PUPPIES	FREE SPACE	CARDS	GATE
HINDLEY	APPLESAUCE	KIDNAP	HEIR	LOCK
LETTERS	HEATHCLIFF	THRUSHCROSS	ZILLAH	SERVANTS

Wuthering Heights

HARETON	PITY	CATHY	CRY	GRAVE
LOVE	NELLY	WILD	PUPPIES	LINTON
CATHERINE	CARDS	FREE SPACE	WUTHERING	FRANCES
REVENGE	EARNSHAW	GATE	KIDNAP	JOSEPH
FIT	LETTERS	COUSIN	ZILLAH	EDGAR

Wuthering Heights

PENISTON	APPLESAUCE	MARRIAGE	SPANIEL	HINDLEY
MORTGAGES	DREAM	LOCK	THRUSHCROSS	BRONTE
SOLITUDE	HEATHCLIFF	FREE SPACE	LOCKWOOD	ISABELLA
SICKLY	HEIR	GUN	GHOST	EDGAR
ZILLAH	COUSIN	LETTERS	FIT	JOSEPH

Wuthering Heights

NELLY	FIT	KIDNAP	HARETON	HINDLEY
SICKLY	LOCKWOOD	CATHY	WUTHERING	SPANIEL
THRUSHCROSS	HEIR	FREE SPACE	SOLITUDE	MORTGAGES
PITY	PENISTON	LOCK	COUSIN	WILD
GHOST	ISABELLA	HEATHCLIFF	FRANCES	CARDS

Wuthering Heights

CRY	JOSEPH	LETTERS	PUPPIES	ZILLAH
BRONTE	LOVE	LINTON	REVENGE	MOOR
EDGAR	EARNSHAW	FREE SPACE	APPLESAUCE	SERVANTS
CATHERINE	MARRIAGE	DREAM	GATE	CARDS
FRANCES	HEATHCLIFF	ISABELLA	GHOST	WILD

Wuthering Heights

FIT	WILD	LINTON	LOCKWOOD	MARRIAGE
HARETON	MORTGAGES	COUSIN	PENISTON	FRANCES
EDGAR	JOSEPH	FREE SPACE	SICKLY	THRUSHCROSS
MOOR	CRY	SERVANTS	PITY	HEIR
APPLESAUCE	EARNSHAW	HEATHCLIFF	SOLITUDE	GHOST

Wuthering Heights

REVENGE	ZILLAH	GRAVE	GATE	ISABELLA
HINDLEY	BRONTE	LETTERS	CATHY	LOVE
DREAM	KIDNAP	FREE SPACE	PUPPIES	WUTHERING
GUN	SPANIEL	CARDS	CATHERINE	GHOST
SOLITUDE	HEATHCLIFF	EARNSHAW	APPLESAUCE	HEIR

Wuthering Heights

HINDLEY	GRAVE	WUTHERING	THRUSHCROSS	NELLY
COUSIN	CRY	MARRIAGE	APPLESAUCE	LOVE
CATHERINE	HEATHCLIFF	FREE SPACE	BRONTE	CATHY
KIDNAP	LETTERS	SICKLY	ISABELLA	LINTON
GUN	EDGAR	CARDS	GATE	LOCK

Wuthering Heights

PENISTON	SPANIEL	HEIR	LOCKWOOD	HARETON
JOSEPH	WILD	GHOST	REVENGE	ZILLAH
MOOR	MORTGAGES	FREE SPACE	DREAM	SERVANTS
FRANCES	EARNSHAW	SOLITUDE	FIT	LOCK
GATE	CARDS	EDGAR	GUN	LINTON

Wuthering Heights

LOCK	MOOR	GUN	SICKLY	ISABELLA
LOVE	APPLESAUCE	CATHERINE	FIT	LINTON
CARDS	GRAVE	FREE SPACE	GHOST	HINDLEY
DREAM	EARNSHAW	GATE	MORTGAGES	WUTHERING
ZILLAH	KIDNAP	NELLY	JOSEPH	PENISTON

Wuthering Heights

HEATHCLIFF	LOCKWOOD	SPANIEL	HARETON	THRUSHCROSS
WILD	REVENGE	EDGAR	CATHY	COUSIN
BRONTE	FRANCES	FREE SPACE	SERVANTS	HEIR
PUPPIES	SOLITUDE	MARRIAGE	LETTERS	PENISTON
JOSEPH	NELLY	KIDNAP	ZILLAH	WUTHERING

Wuthering Heights

HARETON	HEATHCLIFF	PITY	CATHY	LETTERS
NELLY	PENISTON	THRUSHCROSS	SPANIEL	CARDS
SICKLY	LOCK	FREE SPACE	GATE	WILD
COUSIN	HINDLEY	CATHERINE	CRY	ISABELLA
ZILLAH	KIDNAP	EDGAR	MARRIAGE	JOSEPH

Wuthering Heights

BRONTE	APPLESAUCE	SOLITUDE	DREAM	FRANCES
MOOR	GHOST	LOVE	LINTON	LOCKWOOD
WUTHERING	PUPPIES	FREE SPACE	GRAVE	FIT
SERVANTS	REVENGE	HEIR	MORTGAGES	JOSEPH
MARRIAGE	EDGAR	KIDNAP	ZILLAH	ISABELLA

Wuthering Heights

APPLESAUCE	GRAVE	PUPPIES	CARDS	BRONTE
MARRIAGE	FRANCES	HINDLEY	HEIR	HEATHCLIFF
DREAM	CRY	FREE SPACE	PITY	SOLITUDE
EARNSHAW	NELLY	CATHY	MORTGAGES	REVENGE
FIT	GATE	WILD	MOOR	KIDNAP

Wuthering Heights

PENISTON	LETTERS	GHOST	THRUSHCROSS	CATHERINE
JOSEPH	HARETON	LOVE	ISABELLA	LOCKWOOD
SPANIEL	LOCK	FREE SPACE	LINTON	SICKLY
WUTHERING	COUSIN	SERVANTS	EDGAR	KIDNAP
MOOR	WILD	GATE	FIT	REVENGE

Wuthering Heights

LOVE	NELLY	MARRIAGE	ZILLAH	CARDS
SERVANTS	SICKLY	CATHERINE	PENISTON	SPANIEL
CRY	BRONTE	FREE SPACE	APPLESAUCE	HARETON
GUN	HEATHCLIFF	MOOR	PUPPIES	ISABELLA
LOCK	JOSEPH	EARNSHAW	KIDNAP	COUSIN

Wuthering Heights

LETTERS	HEIR	FRANCES	GATE	PITY
WUTHERING	GRAVE	GHOST	FIT	CATHY
DREAM	EDGAR	FREE SPACE	WILD	REVENGE
LINTON	SOLITUDE	THRUSHCROSS	HINDLEY	COUSIN
KIDNAP	EARNSHAW	JOSEPH	LOCK	ISABELLA

Wuthering Heights

SOLITUDE	HINDLEY	PITY	GATE	GUN
THRUSHCROSS	WILD	GHOST	PENISTON	LOCKWOOD
WUTHERING	EDGAR	FREE SPACE	ISABELLA	CARDS
HEATHCLIFF	SICKLY	FIT	MOOR	FRANCES
NELLY	JOSEPH	APPLESAUCE	LETTERS	LINTON

Wuthering Heights

CATHY	CATHERINE	HEIR	LOCK	REVENGE
GRAVE	BRONTE	CRY	ZILLAH	EARNSHAW
MORTGAGES	HARETON	FREE SPACE	SPANIEL	SERVANTS
COUSIN	MARRIAGE	PUPPIES	KIDNAP	LINTON
LETTERS	APPLESAUCE	JOSEPH	NELLY	FRANCES

Wuthering Heights

THRUSHCROSS	PUPPIES	GRAVE	BRONTE	CRY
MORTGAGES	JOSEPH	NELLY	HARETON	SPANIEL
REVENGE	GATE	FREE SPACE	DREAM	MOOR
CARDS	APPLESAUCE	CATHY	LOCK	LETTERS
WUTHERING	FRANCES	WILD	ZILLAH	GHOST

CARD NO: 40

MARY COLLINS

Wuthering Heights

LOCKWOOD	KIDNAP	ISABELLA	FIT	LINTON
HEATHCLIFF	EDGAR	MARRIAGE	GUN	LOVE
HINDLEY	CATHERINE	FREE SPACE	PENISTON	HEIR
EARNSHAW	SICKLY	COUSIN	SOLITUDE	GHOST
ZILLAH	WILD	FRANCES	WUTHERING	LETTERS

Wuthering Heights

GATE	MOOR	KIDNAP	JOSEPH	WUTHERING
ZILLAH	CRY	GRAVE	GUN	PITY
HEIR	FIT	FREE SPACE	EDGAR	GHOST
DREAM	COUSIN	SPANIEL	CATHY	LOVE
SOLITUDE	MARRIAGE	SERVANTS	CATHERINE	PENISTON

Wuthering Heights

WILD	LINTON	SICKLY	NELLY	FRANCES
EARNSHAW	LOCKWOOD	LETTERS	BRONTE	CARDS
HARETON	REVENGE	FREE SPACE	THRUSHCROSS	LOCK
ISABELLA	HEATHCLIFF	APPLESAUCE	PUPPIES	PENISTON
CATHERINE	SERVANTS	MARRIAGE	SOLITUDE	LOVE

Wuthering Heights

MORTGAGES	GRAVE	FRANCES	MARRIAGE	KIDNAP
GHOST	MOOR	NELLY	APPLESAUCE	FIT
HARETON	SPANIEL	FREE SPACE	EDGAR	WUTHERING
LOCKWOOD	HINDLEY	LINTON	ZILLAH	EARNSHAW
CATHERINE	HEATHCLIFF	SICKLY	GUN	LOVE

Wuthering Heights

DREAM	SOLITUDE	JOSEPH	PITY	SERVANTS
CATHY	CARDS	THRUSHCROSS	GATE	ISABELLA
CRY	LOCK	FREE SPACE	HEIR	REVENGE
BRONTE	PUPPIES	LETTERS	WILD	LOVE
GUN	SICKLY	HEATHCLIFF	CATHERINE	EARNSHAW

Wuthering Heights Vocabulary Word List

No.	Word	Clue/Definition
1.	ABETTED	Encouraged
2.	ACQUIESCED	Consented
3.	ADMONITION	Advice
4.	ADROITLY	Cleverly; deftly
5.	AFFIRMING	Asserting; maintaining
6.	AGHAST	Astonished
7.	ALLY	Collaborator; partner
8.	AMIABLE	Good-natured
9.	ANNIHILATE	Obliterate
10.	APPALL	Dismay
11.	ASSERTION	Statement
12.	AVERTED	Turned away
13.	CANDID	Frank
14.	CAPRICES	Whims
15.	COGITATIONS	Thoughts
16.	COMPULSORY	Mandatory; involuntary
17.	CONDESCENDING	Patronizing
18.	CONJECTURE	Suppose
19.	CONSPIRE	Scheme
20.	CONTRADICT	Dispute; oppose
21.	CONTRITE	Apologetic
22.	CONTRIVE	Devise; find a way
23.	CORDIAL	Congenial; friendly
24.	COUNTENANCE	Facial expression
25.	DECEIT	Deception
26.	DEFY	Challenge
27.	DEGRADATION	Disgrace
28.	DELIRIUM	Madness caused by illness
29.	DELUDED	Deceived; fooled
30.	DESPONDENCY	Discouragement
31.	DISCERNED	Perceived
32.	EMULOUS	Eager to equal or surpass another
33.	ENDURE	Tolerate
34.	ENSCONCING	Settling comfortably
35.	EVINCED	Revealed
36.	EXASPERATE	Infuriate
37.	EXPOSTULATING	Reasoning to dissuade or correct
38.	FEIGNED	Pretend
39.	FOES	Enemies
40.	FRET	Worry
41.	HYPOCRITE	Deceiver
42.	IDLE	Lazy; inactive
43.	IMPERTINENCE	Impudence
44.	INDIGNATION	Resentment
45.	INDULGENT	Obliging; lenient
46.	INSOLENCE	Presumptuous and insulting in manner or speech
47.	INTERLOPER	Intruder
48.	INTRACTABLE	Uncontrollable
49.	LETHARGY	Listlessness
50.	LEVITY	Flippancy
51.	MAGNANIMITY	Nobility; graciousness

Wuthering Heights Vocabulary Word List Cont.

No.	Word	Clue/Definition
52.	MANIFESTED	Exhibited
53.	MISANTHROPIST	Person who hates mankind
54.	MITIGATED	Moderated
55.	MORTIFICATION	Embarrassment
56.	OBLIGE	Accommodate
57.	OBVIATE	Prevent difficulties by effective measures
58.	ODIOUS	Detestable
59.	ORISONS	Prayers
60.	PEEVISH	Irritable
61.	PERPETUAL	Continuous; endless
62.	PERSEVERED	Persisted
63.	PERUSED	Read
64.	PETULANCE	Unreasonable ill temper
65.	PLIGHT	Situation; condition
66.	PORTENDED	Forecast
67.	PRECEDE	Go before
68.	PRETENSE	False appearance or action
69.	PROPENSITY	Tendency
70.	PROVINCIALISMS	Manners unfashionable or unsophisticated
71.	RECIPROCATION	Return
72.	RECOMPENSE	Payment
73.	RECONCILED	Reunited
74.	SANGUINE	Optimistic
75.	SANCTIMONIOUS	Self-righteous
76.	SATURNINE	Sullen
77.	SCRUTINIZING	Inspecting
78.	SUSCEPTIBLE	Vulnerable
79.	TREPIDATION	Apprehension
80.	VANQUISH	Overpower
81.	VEXED	Annoyed
82.	VINDICTIVENESS	Spitefulness
83.	VIVACITY	Energy

Wuthering Heights Vocabulary Fill In The Blanks 1

_____ 1. Facial expression

_____ 2. Impudence

_____ 3. Reasoning to dissuade or correct

_____ 4. Mandatory; involuntary

_____ 5. Detestable

_____ 6. Collaborator; partner

_____ 7. Challenge

_____ 8. Cleverly; deftly

_____ 9. Apprehension

_____ 10. Whims

_____ 11. False appearance or action

_____ 12. Manners unfashionable or unsophisticated

_____ 13. Settling comfortably

_____ 14. Intruder

_____ 15. Devise; find a way

_____ 16. Resentment

_____ 17. Presumptuous and insulting in manner or speech

_____ 18. Listlessness

_____ 19. Embarrassment

_____ 20. Obliging; lenient

Wuthering Heights Vocabulary Fill In The Blanks 1 Answer Key

COUNTENANCE	1. Facial expression
IMPERTINENCE	2. Impudence
EXPOSTULATING	3. Reasoning to dissuade or correct
COMPULSORY	4. Mandatory; involuntary
ODIOUS	5. Detestable
ALLY	6. Collaborator; partner
DEFY	7. Challenge
ADROITLY	8. Cleverly; deftly
TREPIDATION	9. Apprehension
CAPRICES	10. Whims
PRETENSE	11. False appearance or action
PROVINCIALISMS	12. Manners unfashionable or unsophisticated
ENSCONCING	13. Settling comfortably
INTERLOPER	14. Intruder
CONTRIVE	15. Devise; find a way
INDIGNATION	16. Resentment
INSOLENCE	17. Presumptuous and insulting in manner or speech
LETHARGY	18. Listlessness
MORTIFICATION	19. Embarrassment
INDULGENT	20. Obliging; lenient

Wuthering Heights Vocabulary Fill In The Blanks 2

_____   1. Asserting; maintaining
_____   2. Pretend
_____   3. Exhibited
_____   4. Listlessness
_____   5. Consented
_____   6. Impudence
_____   7. Thoughts
_____   8. Reasoning to dissuade or correct
_____   9. Continuous; endless
_____   10. Self-righteous
_____   11. Good-natured
_____   12. Whims
_____   13. Congenial; friendly
_____   14. Moderated
_____   15. Discouragement
_____   16. Situation; condition
_____   17. Energy
_____   18. Apologetic
_____   19. Uncontrollable
_____   20. Cleverly; deftly

Wuthering Heights Vocabulary Fill In The Blanks 2 Answer Key

AFFIRMING	1. Asserting; maintaining
FEIGNED	2. Pretend
MANIFESTED	3. Exhibited
LETHARGY	4. Listlessness
ACQUIESCED	5. Consented
IMPERTINENCE	6. Impudence
COGITATIONS	7. Thoughts
EXPOSTULATING	8. Reasoning to dissuade or correct
PERPETUAL	9. Continuous; endless
SANCTIMONIOUS	10. Self-righteous
AMIABLE	11. Good-natured
CAPRICES	12. Whims
CORDIAL	13. Congenial; friendly
MITIGATED	14. Moderated
DESPONDENCY	15. Discouragement
PLIGHT	16. Situation; condition
VIVACITY	17. Energy
CONTRITE	18. Apologetic
INTRACTABLE	19. Uncontrollable
ADROITLY	20. Cleverly; deftly

Wuthering Heights Vocabulary Fill In The Blanks 3

_____ 1. Encouraged

_____ 2. Presumptuous and insulting in manner or speech

_____ 3. Deceiver

_____ 4. Forecast

_____ 5. Turned away

_____ 6. Scheme

_____ 7. Go before

_____ 8. Eager to equal or surpass another

_____ 9. Exhibited

_____ 10. Infuriate

_____ 11. Intruder

_____ 12. Apprehension

_____ 13. Pretend

_____ 14. Suppose

_____ 15. Statement

_____ 16. Devise; find a way

_____ 17. Impudence

_____ 18. Revealed

_____ 19. Dispute; oppose

_____ 20. Thoughts

Wuthering Heights Vocabulary Fill In The Blanks 3 Answer Key

ABETTED   1. Encouraged
INSOLENCE   2. Presumptuous and insulting in manner or speech
HYPOCRITE   3. Deceiver
PORTENDED   4. Forecast
AVERTED   5. Turned away
CONSPIRE   6. Scheme
PRECEDE   7. Go before
EMULOUS   8. Eager to equal or surpass another
MANIFESTED   9. Exhibited
EXASPERATE   10. Infuriate
INTERLOPER   11. Intruder
TREPIDATION   12. Apprehension
FEIGNED   13. Pretend
CONJECTURE   14. Suppose
ASSERTION   15. Statement
CONTRIVE   16. Devise; find a way
IMPERTINENCE   17. Impudence
EVINCED   18. Revealed
CONTRADICT   19. Dispute; oppose
COGITATIONS   20. Thoughts

Wuthering Heights Vocabulary Fill In The Blanks 4

_____ 1. Revealed

_____ 2. Dispute; oppose

_____ 3. Deception

_____ 4. Scheme

_____ 5. Embarrassment

_____ 6. Inspecting

_____ 7. Settling comfortably

_____ 8. Energy

_____ 9. Moderated

_____ 10. Annoyed

_____ 11. Manners unfashionable or unsophisticated

_____ 12. Go before

_____ 13. Reasoning to dissuade or correct

_____ 14. False appearance or action

_____ 15. Payment

_____ 16. Reunited

_____ 17. Consented

_____ 18. Apprehension

_____ 19. Whims

_____ 20. Eager to equal or surpass another

Wuthering Heights Vocabulary Fill In The Blanks 4 Answer Key

EVINCED	1.	Revealed
CONTRADICT	2.	Dispute; oppose
DECEIT	3.	Deception
CONSPIRE	4.	Scheme
MORTIFICATION	5.	Embarrassment
SCRUTINIZING	6.	Inspecting
ENSCONCING	7.	Settling comfortably
VIVACITY	8.	Energy
MITIGATED	9.	Moderated
VEXED	10.	Annoyed
PROVINCIALISMS	11.	Manners unfashionable or unsophisticated
PRECEDE	12.	Go before
EXPOSTULATING	13.	Reasoning to dissuade or correct
PRETENSE	14.	False appearance or action
RECOMPENSE	15.	Payment
RECONCILED	16.	Reunited
ACQUIESCED	17.	Consented
TREPIDATION	18.	Apprehension
CAPRICES	19.	Whims
EMULOUS	20.	Eager to equal or surpass another

Wuthering Heights Matching 1

___ 1. CONSPIRE   A. Payment
___ 2. MITIGATED   B. Disgrace
___ 3. DISCERNED   C. Uncontrollable
___ 4. INTRACTABLE   D. Devise; find a way
___ 5. INSOLENCE   E. Irritable
___ 6. CONTRIVE   F. Revealed
___ 7. RECOMPENSE   G. Perceived
___ 8. FOES   H. Consented
___ 9. CONTRITE   I. Intruder
___10. PRECEDE   J. Deceived; fooled
___11. ACQUIESCED   K. Moderated
___12. HYPOCRITE   L. Cleverly; deftly
___13. ADMONITION   M. Astonished
___14. INTERLOPER   N. Enemies
___15. OBVIATE   O. Prevent difficulties by effective measures
___16. DELUDED   P. Accommodate
___17. EXPOSTULATING   Q. Go before
___18. OBLIGE   R. Reasoning to dissuade or correct
___19. DEGRADATION   S. Tendency
___20. PROPENSITY   T. Apologetic
___21. ADROITLY   U. Scheme
___22. EVINCED   V. Deceiver
___23. PEEVISH   W. Inspecting
___24. AGHAST   X. Advice
___25. SCRUTINIZING   Y. Presumptuous and insulting in manner or speech

Wuthering Heights Matching 1 Answer Key

U - 1. CONSPIRE	A. Payment
K - 2. MITIGATED	B. Disgrace
G - 3. DISCERNED	C. Uncontrollable
C - 4. INTRACTABLE	D. Devise; find a way
Y - 5. INSOLENCE	E. Irritable
D - 6. CONTRIVE	F. Revealed
A - 7. RECOMPENSE	G. Perceived
N - 8. FOES	H. Consented
T - 9. CONTRITE	I. Intruder
Q - 10. PRECEDE	J. Deceived; fooled
H - 11. ACQUIESCED	K. Moderated
V - 12. HYPOCRITE	L. Cleverly; deftly
X - 13. ADMONITION	M. Astonished
I - 14. INTERLOPER	N. Enemies
O - 15. OBVIATE	O. Prevent difficulties by effective measures
J - 16. DELUDED	P. Accommodate
R - 17. EXPOSTULATING	Q. Go before
P - 18. OBLIGE	R. Reasoning to dissuade or correct
B - 19. DEGRADATION	S. Tendency
S - 20. PROPENSITY	T. Apologetic
L - 21. ADROITLY	U. Scheme
F - 22. EVINCED	V. Deceiver
E - 23. PEEVISH	W. Inspecting
M - 24. AGHAST	X. Advice
W - 25. SCRUTINIZING	Y. Presumptuous and insulting in manner or speech

Wuthering Heights Matching 2

___ 1. CAPRICES   A. Moderated
___ 2. INSOLENCE   B. Astonished
___ 3. ODIOUS   C. Cleverly; deftly
___ 4. PROVINCIALISMS   D. Presumptuous and insulting in manner or speech
___ 5. AGHAST   E. Flippancy
___ 6. LEVITY   F. Apologetic
___ 7. MITIGATED   G. Irritable
___ 8. PROPENSITY   H. Discouragement
___ 9. LETHARGY   I. Situation; condition
___10. COGITATIONS   J. Thoughts
___11. PERUSED   K. Uncontrollable
___12. CORDIAL   L. Statement
___13. VIVACITY   M. Reasoning to dissuade or correct
___14. ADROITLY   N. Listlessness
___15. PLIGHT   O. Manners unfashionable or unsophisticated
___16. CONTRITE   P. Spitefulness
___17. EVINCED   Q. Energy
___18. INTRACTABLE   R. Congenial; friendly
___19. DEGRADATION   S. Revealed
___20. DESPONDENCY   T. Deceived; fooled
___21. EXPOSTULATING   U. Whims
___22. PEEVISH   V. Disgrace
___23. DELUDED   W. Read
___24. ASSERTION   X. Detestable
___25. VINDICTIVENESS   Y. Tendency

Wuthering Heights Matching 2 Answer Key

U - 1.	CAPRICES	A. Moderated
D - 2.	INSOLENCE	B. Astonished
X - 3.	ODIOUS	C. Cleverly; deftly
O - 4.	PROVINCIALISMS	D. Presumptuous and insulting in manner or speech
B - 5.	AGHAST	E. Flippancy
E - 6.	LEVITY	F. Apologetic
A - 7.	MITIGATED	G. Irritable
Y - 8.	PROPENSITY	H. Discouragement
N - 9.	LETHARGY	I. Situation; condition
J - 10.	COGITATIONS	J. Thoughts
W - 11.	PERUSED	K. Uncontrollable
R - 12.	CORDIAL	L. Statement
Q - 13.	VIVACITY	M. Reasoning to dissuade or correct
C - 14.	ADROITLY	N. Listlessness
I - 15.	PLIGHT	O. Manners unfashionable or unsophisticated
F - 16.	CONTRITE	P. Spitefulness
S - 17.	EVINCED	Q. Energy
K - 18.	INTRACTABLE	R. Congenial; friendly
V - 19.	DEGRADATION	S. Revealed
H - 20.	DESPONDENCY	T. Deceived; fooled
M - 21.	EXPOSTULATING	U. Whims
G - 22.	PEEVISH	V. Disgrace
T - 23.	DELUDED	W. Read
L - 24.	ASSERTION	X. Detestable
P - 25.	VINDICTIVENESS	Y. Tendency

Wuthering Heights Matching 3

___ 1. AGHAST   A. Inspecting
___ 2. PRETENSE   B. Challenge
___ 3. INSOLENCE   C. Presumptuous and insulting in manner or speech
___ 4. VANQUISH   D. Exhibited
___ 5. RECIPROCATION   E. Devise; find a way
___ 6. RECOMPENSE   F. Tendency
___ 7. MORTIFICATION   G. Return
___ 8. PROPENSITY   H. Advice
___ 9. ALLY   I. Annoyed
___ 10. IMPERTINENCE   J. Payment
___ 11. CONTRIVE   K. Perceived
___ 12. OBLIGE   L. Accommodate
___ 13. ADMONITION   M. Astonished
___ 14. LEVITY   N. Collaborator; partner
___ 15. ASSERTION   O. Nobility; graciousness
___ 16. IDLE   P. Embarrassment
___ 17. DISCERNED   Q. Lazy; inactive
___ 18. VEXED   R. Uncontrollable
___ 19. MANIFESTED   S. False appearance or action
___ 20. MAGNANIMITY   T. Overpower
___ 21. PLIGHT   U. Situation; condition
___ 22. SCRUTINIZING   V. Continuous; endless
___ 23. DEFY   W. Impudence
___ 24. PERPETUAL   X. Flippancy
___ 25. INTRACTABLE   Y. Statement

Wuthering Heights Matching 3 Answer Key

M - 1. AGHAST	A.	Inspecting
S - 2. PRETENSE	B.	Challenge
C - 3. INSOLENCE	C.	Presumptuous and insulting in manner or speech
T - 4. VANQUISH	D.	Exhibited
G - 5. RECIPROCATION	E.	Devise; find a way
J - 6. RECOMPENSE	F.	Tendency
P - 7. MORTIFICATION	G.	Return
F - 8. PROPENSITY	H.	Advice
N - 9. ALLY	I.	Annoyed
W - 10. IMPERTINENCE	J.	Payment
E - 11. CONTRIVE	K.	Perceived
L - 12. OBLIGE	L.	Accommodate
H - 13. ADMONITION	M.	Astonished
X - 14. LEVITY	N.	Collaborator; partner
Y - 15. ASSERTION	O.	Nobility; graciousness
Q - 16. IDLE	P.	Embarrassment
K - 17. DISCERNED	Q.	Lazy; inactive
I - 18. VEXED	R.	Uncontrollable
D - 19. MANIFESTED	S.	False appearance or action
O - 20. MAGNANIMITY	T.	Overpower
U - 21. PLIGHT	U.	Situation; condition
A - 22. SCRUTINIZING	V.	Continuous; endless
B - 23. DEFY	W.	Impudence
V - 24. PERPETUAL	X.	Flippancy
R - 25. INTRACTABLE	Y.	Statement

Wuthering Heights Matching 4

___ 1. DEFY   A. Deception
___ 2. FRET   B. Read
___ 3. RECOMPENSE   C. Situation; condition
___ 4. CONDESCENDING D. Uncontrollable
___ 5. PORTENDED   E. Challenge
___ 6. DESPONDENCY   F. Forecast
___ 7. ANNIHILATE   G. Cleverly; deftly
___ 8. PERUSED   H. Revealed
___ 9. INTRACTABLE   I. Asserting; maintaining
___ 10. PLIGHT   J. Worry
___ 11. MANIFESTED   K. Consented
___ 12. CONTRADICT   L. Discouragement
___ 13. EVINCED   M. Spitefulness
___ 14. HYPOCRITE   N. Whims
___ 15. ACQUIESCED   O. Deceiver
___ 16. PROPENSITY   P. Dispute; oppose
___ 17. ADROITLY   Q. Exhibited
___ 18. IDLE   R. Lazy; inactive
___ 19. DECEIT   S. Continuous; endless
___ 20. AFFIRMING   T. Obliterate
___ 21. VINDICTIVENESS U. Enemies
___ 22. FOES   V. Patronizing
___ 23. VANQUISH   W. Payment
___ 24. CAPRICES   X. Overpower
___ 25. PERPETUAL   Y. Tendency

Wuthering Heights Matching 4 Answer Key

E - 1. DEFY		A. Deception
J - 2. FRET		B. Read
W - 3. RECOMPENSE		C. Situation; condition
V - 4. CONDESCENDING		D. Uncontrollable
F - 5. PORTENDED		E. Challenge
L - 6. DESPONDENCY		F. Forecast
T - 7. ANNIHILATE		G. Cleverly; deftly
B - 8. PERUSED		H. Revealed
D - 9. INTRACTABLE		I. Asserting; maintaining
C - 10. PLIGHT		J. Worry
Q - 11. MANIFESTED		K. Consented
P - 12. CONTRADICT		L. Discouragement
H - 13. EVINCED		M. Spitefulness
O - 14. HYPOCRITE		N. Whims
K - 15. ACQUIESCED		O. Deceiver
Y - 16. PROPENSITY		P. Dispute; oppose
G - 17. ADROITLY		Q. Exhibited
R - 18. IDLE		R. Lazy; inactive
A - 19. DECEIT		S. Continuous; endless
I - 20. AFFIRMING		T. Obliterate
M - 21. VINDICTIVENESS		U. Enemies
U - 22. FOES		V. Patronizing
X - 23. VANQUISH		W. Payment
N - 24. CAPRICES		X. Overpower
S - 25. PERPETUAL		Y. Tendency

Wuthering Heights Vocabulary Magic Squares 1

Match the definition with the vocabulary word. Put your answers in the magic squares below. When your answers are correct, all columns and rows will add to the same number.

A. ASSERTION
B. LEVITY
C. PETULANCE
D. PRECEDE
E. AMIABLE
F. FEIGNED

G. SUSCEPTIBLE
H. AGHAST
I. SANGUINE
J. PEEVISH
K. VANQUISH
L. IMPERTINENCE

M. EMULOUS
N. VIVACITY
O. CANDID
P. CONJECTURE

1. Eager to equal or surpass another
2. Pretend
3. Astonished
4. Frank
5. Impudence
6. Unreasonable ill temper
7. Statement
8. Irritable
9. Overpower
10. Go before
11. Flippancy
12. Optimistic
13. Energy
14. Good-natured
15. Vulnerable
16. Suppose

A=	B=	C=	D=
E=	F=	G=	H=
I=	J=	K=	L=
M=	N=	O=	P=

Wuthering Heights Vocabulary Magic Squares 1 Answer Key

Match the definition with the vocabulary word. Put your answers in the magic squares below. When your answers are correct, all columns and rows will add to the same number.

A. ASSERTION
B. LEVITY
C. PETULANCE
D. PRECEDE
E. AMIABLE
F. FEIGNED

G. SUSCEPTIBLE
H. AGHAST
I. SANGUINE
J. PEEVISH
K. VANQUISH
L. IMPERTINENCE

M. EMULOUS
N. VIVACITY
O. CANDID
P. CONJECTURE

1. Eager to equal or surpass another
2. Pretend
3. Astonished
4. Frank
5. Impudence
6. Unreasonable ill temper
7. Statement
8. Irritable
9. Overpower
10. Go before
11. Flippancy
12. Optimistic
13. Energy
14. Good-natured
15. Vulnerable
16. Suppose

A=7	B=11	C=6	D=10
E=14	F=2	G=15	H=3
I=12	J=8	K=9	L=5
M=1	N=13	O=4	P=16

Wuthering Heights Vocabulary Magic Squares 2

Match the definition with the vocabulary word. Put your answers in the magic squares below. When your answers are correct, all columns and rows will add to the same number.

A. CONTRIVE
B. INDIGNATION
C. VIVACITY
D. PORTENDED
E. COMPULSORY
F. PRECEDE
G. INDULGENT
H. FEIGNED
I. MITIGATED
J. AFFIRMING
K. ASSERTION
L. OBLIGE
M. DECEIT
N. ADMONITION
O. RECOMPENSE
P. CORDIAL

1. Resentment
2. Obliging; lenient
3. Statement
4. Advice
5. Deception
6. Accommodate
7. Pretend
8. Devise; find a way
9. Congenial; friendly
10. Moderated
11. Mandatory; involuntary
12. Forecast
13. Energy
14. Go before
15. Asserting; maintaining
16. Payment

A=	B=	C=	D=
E=	F=	G=	H=
I=	J=	K=	L=
M=	N=	O=	P=

Wuthering Heights Vocabulary Magic Squares 2 Answer Key

Match the definition with the vocabulary word. Put your answers in the magic squares below. When your answers are correct, all columns and rows will add to the same number.

A. CONTRIVE
B. INDIGNATION
C. VIVACITY
D. PORTENDED
E. COMPULSORY
F. PRECEDE
G. INDULGENT
H. FEIGNED
I. MITIGATED
J. AFFIRMING
K. ASSERTION
L. OBLIGE
M. DECEIT
N. ADMONITION
O. RECOMPENSE
P. CORDIAL

1. Resentment
2. Obliging; lenient
3. Statement
4. Advice
5. Deception
6. Accommodate
7. Pretend
8. Devise; find a way
9. Congenial; friendly
10. Moderated
11. Mandatory; involuntary
12. Forecast
13. Energy
14. Go before
15. Asserting; maintaining
16. Payment

A=8	B=1	C=13	D=12
E=11	F=14	G=2	H=7
I=10	J=15	K=3	L=6
M=5	N=4	O=16	P=9

82 Copyright 2005 Teacher's Pet Publications

Wuthering Heights Vocabulary Magic Squares 3

Match the definition with the vocabulary word. Put your answers in the magic squares below. When your answers are correct, all columns and rows will add to the same number.

A. PROVINCIALISMS
B. ASSERTION
C. ENSCONCING
D. MISANTHROPIST
E. COUNTENANCE
F. COMPULSORY
G. PROPENSITY
H. ANNIHILATE
I. AFFIRMING
J. EMULOUS
K. SCRUTINIZING
L. SUSCEPTIBLE
M. PEEVISH
N. ODIOUS
O. PERPETUAL
P. AVERTED

1. Obliterate
2. Manners unfashionable or unsophisticated
3. Statement
4. Tendency
5. Eager to equal or surpass another
6. Continuous; endless
7. Turned away
8. Asserting; maintaining
9. Inspecting
10. Detestable
11. Irritable
12. Vulnerable
13. Facial expression
14. Person who hates mankind
15. Settling comfortably
16. Mandatory; involuntary

A=	B=	C=	D=
E=	F=	G=	H=
I=	J=	K=	L=
M=	N=	O=	P=

Wuthering Heights Vocabulary Magic Squares 3 Answer Key

Match the definition with the vocabulary word. Put your answers in the magic squares below. When your answers are correct, all columns and rows will add to the same number.

A. PROVINCIALISMS
B. ASSERTION
C. ENSCONCING
D. MISANTHROPIST
E. COUNTENANCE
F. COMPULSORY
G. PROPENSITY
H. ANNIHILATE
I. AFFIRMING
J. EMULOUS
K. SCRUTINIZING
L. SUSCEPTIBLE
M. PEEVISH
N. ODIOUS
O. PERPETUAL
P. AVERTED

1. Obliterate
2. Manners unfashionable or unsophisticated
3. Statement
4. Tendency
5. Eager to equal or surpass another
6. Continuous; endless
7. Turned away
8. Asserting; maintaining
9. Inspecting
10. Detestable
11. Irritable
12. Vulnerable
13. Facial expression
14. Person who hates mankind
15. Settling comfortably
16. Mandatory; involuntary

A=2	B=3	C=15	D=14
E=13	F=16	G=4	H=1
I=8	J=5	K=9	L=12
M=11	N=10	O=6	P=7

Wuthering Heights Vocabulary Magic Squares 4

Match the definition with the vocabulary word. Put your answers in the magic squares below. When your answers are correct, all columns and rows will add to the same number.

A. CANDID
B. DELUDED
C. DELIRIUM
D. HYPOCRITE
E. FOES
F. PLIGHT
G. MORTIFICATION
H. AMIABLE
I. RECIPROCATION
J. OBVIATE
K. ENDURE
L. SATURNINE
M. ADROITLY
N. VEXED
O. CONTRIVE
P. COMPULSORY

1. Frank
2. Annoyed
3. Prevent difficulties by effective measures
4. Enemies
5. Embarrassment
6. Sullen
7. Mandatory; involuntary
8. Madness caused by illness
9. Devise; find a way
10. Deceiver
11. Good-natured
12. Tolerate
13. Return
14. Situation; condition
15. Deceived; fooled
16. Cleverly; deftly

A=	B=	C=	D=
E=	F=	G=	H=
I=	J=	K=	L=
M=	N=	O=	P=

Wuthering Heights Vocabulary Magic Squares 4 Answer Key

Match the definition with the vocabulary word. Put your answers in the magic squares below. When your answers are correct, all columns and rows will add to the same number.

A. CANDID
B. DELUDED
C. DELIRIUM
D. HYPOCRITE
E. FOES
F. PLIGHT
G. MORTIFICATION
H. AMIABLE
I. RECIPROCATION
J. OBVIATE
K. ENDURE
L. SATURNINE
M. ADROITLY
N. VEXED
O. CONTRIVE
P. COMPULSORY

1. Frank
2. Annoyed
3. Prevent difficulties by effective measures
4. Enemies
5. Embarrassment
6. Sullen
7. Mandatory; involuntary
8. Madness caused by illness
9. Devise; find a way
10. Deceiver
11. Good-natured
12. Tolerate
13. Return
14. Situation; condition
15. Deceived; fooled
16. Cleverly; deftly

A=1	B=15	C=8	D=10
E=4	F=14	G=5	H=11
I=13	J=3	K=12	L=6
M=16	N=2	O=9	P=7

Wuthering Heights Vocabulary Word Search 1

```
C A P R I C E S N P V S E D R I M D F Q
B D E B Q D O H E G S L A E V N C E E H
P M E H X E Z R N W D F M X T T S C I N
O O V W K T U C D I F D M E N E P E G L
R N I S M S I L A I C N I V O R P I N T
T I S D E E M Q R N A S L F E L E T E L
E T H D V F D M V D L L R T I O R C D R
N I L G K I I A A U W E E G P P P O E Y
D O Q W D N L L N L T N H Z R E E N T G
E N C N G A G L Q G S T Z O E R T T T L
D Q A O L M O Y U E C D P A C S U R E J
E C L B N B L F I N O E E M E E A I B B
C C L V L T F E S T N T T I D V L T A Q
S N M I E C R D H S T A U A E E P E K P
E H G A M S D I I K R G L B V R H Y Y F
I E W T U Z L T V N A I A L I E H Y T K
U Y D E L B Y N J E D T N E N D R T I V
Q A D R O I T L Y K I I C P C C B T V S
C O M P U L S O R Y C M E D E L U D E D
A O R I S O N S R D T F E N D U R E L D
```

Accommodate (6)
Advice (10)
Annoyed (5)
Apologetic (8)
Asserting; maintaining (9)
Challenge (4)
Cleverly; deftly (8)
Collaborator; partner (4)
Congenial; friendly (7)
Consented (10)
Continuous; endless (9)
Deceived; fooled (7)
Deception (6)
Devise; find a way (8)
Dispute; oppose (10)
Eager to equal or surpass another (7)
Encouraged (7)
Enemies (4)
Exhibited (10)
False appearance or action (8)
Flippancy (6)
Forecast (9)
Frank (6)
Go before (7)

Good-natured (7)
Intruder (10)
Irritable (7)
Lazy; inactive (4)
Mandatory; involuntary (10)
Manners unfashionable or unsophisticated (14)
Moderated (9)
Obliging; lenient (9)
Overpower (8)
Persisted (10)
Prayers (7)
Pretend (7)
Prevent difficulties by effective measures (7)
Read (7)
Revealed (7)
Situation; condition (6)
Tendency (10)
Tolerate (6)
Turned away (7)
Unreasonable ill temper (9)
Whims (8)
Worry (4)

Wuthering Heights Vocabulary Word Search 1 Answer Key

```
C  A  P  R  I  C  E  S     P           E  D        I        D  F
   D  E        D  O     E        L     A  E        N        E  E
P  M  E        E     R     D  F        X     T     S  C     I
O  O  V        T  U     D  I  F        E     E  P  E  G
R  N  I  S  M  S  I  L  A  I  C  N  I  V  O  R  P  I  N
T  I  S     E  E     R  N  A        F  E  L  E  T  E
E  T  H  D     F  D  M  V  D     L  R  T  I  O  R  C  D
N  I        I  I  A  A  U        E  E  G  P  P  P  O  E
D  O     D  N     L  N  L  T  N  H     R  E  E  N  T
E  N  C  N  G  A     L  Q  G  S  T     O  E  R  T  T
D     A  O     M  O  Y  U  E  C  D  P  A  C  S  U  R  E
E  C     B  N  B     F  I  N  O  E  E  M  E  E  A  I  B
C     V  L  T     E  S  T  N  T  T  I  D  V  L  T  A
S     I  E     R  D  H  S  T  A  U  A  E  E     E     Y
E  G  A  M     I  I        R  G  L  B  V  R
I  E     T  U        T  V     A  I  A  L  I  E        T
U     E  L     Y        E  D  T  N  E  N  D  R        I
Q  A  D  R  O  I  T  L  Y        I  I  C     C        T  V
C  O  M  P  U  L  S  O  R  Y  C  M  E  D  E  L  U  D  E  D
A  O  R  I  S  O  N  S           T     E  N  D  U  R  E  L  D
```

Accommodate (6)
Advice (10)
Annoyed (5)
Apologetic (8)
Asserting; maintaining (9)
Challenge (4)
Cleverly; deftly (8)
Collaborator; partner (4)
Congenial; friendly (7)
Consented (10)
Continuous; endless (9)
Deceived; fooled (7)
Deception (6)
Devise; find a way (8)
Dispute; oppose (10)
Eager to equal or surpass another (7)
Encouraged (7)
Enemies (4)
Exhibited (10)
False appearance or action (8)
Flippancy (6)
Forecast (9)
Frank (6)
Go before (7)

Good-natured (7)
Intruder (10)
Irritable (7)
Lazy; inactive (4)
Mandatory; involuntary (10)
Manners unfashionable or unsophisticated (14)
Moderated (9)
Obliging; lenient (9)
Overpower (8)
Persisted (10)
Prayers (7)
Pretend (7)
Prevent difficulties by effective measures (7)
Read (7)
Revealed (7)
Situation; condition (6)
Tendency (10)
Tolerate (6)
Turned away (7)
Unreasonable ill temper (9)
Whims (8)
Worry (4)

Wuthering Heights Vocabulary Word Search 2

```
P L I G H T E N S C O N C I N G N H E M
O E E F E I G N E D W O D E T O S L X Z
R V T I S N S P S C U E G N I I B C A L
I A I U N C D T S N F I W T U A A A S F
S D R N L S Z U T Y L L A Q I D B N P C
O M T H D A O E R B P D N M Y E E D E J
N O N Y B I N L O E I A A D S L T I R K
S N O P D A C C E P V S H E R U T D A M
P I C O N E N T E N P R E C E D E B T L
O T Q C M S M R I X C A Z E C E D C E W
R I E R U L T U X V G E R I O D C Z V P
T O G I I F E V L H E T Q T M A Y D E Q
E N J T R T W V A O D N J S P P D E F B
N D F E I P Z S I J U J E R E B V S A L
D E Z O L D T Z D T N S I S N I M U V Z
E C F L E T H A R G Y C O N S P I R E L
D N M X D S H N O Q E J Y H E J Y E R R
H I E H L P R J C S O B V I A T E P T D
T V S A N C T I M O N I O U S I D L E V
D E M A G N A N I M I T Y F R E T Q D L
```

Accommodate (6)
Advice (10)
Annoyed (5)
Apologetic (8)
Apprehension (11)
Astonished (6)
Challenge (4)
Collaborator; partner (4)
Congenial; friendly (7)
Deceived; fooled (7)
Deceiver (9)
Deception (6)
Detestable (6)
Eager to equal or surpass another (7)
Encouraged (7)
Enemies (4)
Facial expression (11)
Flippancy (6)
Forecast (9)
Frank (6)
Go before (7)
Good-natured (7)
Infuriate (10)
Irritable (7)

Lazy; inactive (4)
Listlessness (8)
Madness caused by illness (8)
Nobility; graciousness (11)
Overpower (8)
Payment (10)
Prayers (7)
Presumptuous and insulting in manner or speech (9)
Pretend (7)
Prevent difficulties by effective measures (7)
Read (7)
Revealed (7)
Scheme (8)
Self-righteous (13)
Settling comfortably (10)
Situation; condition (6)
Spitefulness (14)
Tolerate (6)
Turned away (7)
Unreasonable ill temper (9)
Whims (8)
Worry (4)

Wuthering Heights Vocabulary Word Search 2 Answer Key

```
P L I G H T E N S C O N C I N G N H E
O E E F E I G N E D   O D E   O S L X
R V T I   N           U E G   I B C A
I A I U N   D   S N F I   T U A A A S
S D R N L S   U T Y L L A Q I D B N P
O M T H D A O E R B   D N M   E E D E
N O N Y   I N L O E I A A D   L T I R
S N O P D A C C E P V       E R U T A
P I C O N E   T E N P R E C E D E   T
O T   C M   M R I   C A   E C E D   E
R I E R U L T U   V G E   I O D C     P
T O   I I   E L H E   N   T M A   D E
E N   T R     V A O   N     P     E
N D F E I     S I   U E R E   V S A
D E   O L D T   D T   S I S N   U V
E C   L E T H A R G Y C O N S P I R E
D N   X D S     O   E     H E   E R T
  I E           C S O B V I A T E P T
  V S A N C T I M O N I O U S I D L E
  E M A G N A N I M I T Y F R E T   D
```

Accommodate (6)
Advice (10)
Annoyed (5)
Apologetic (8)
Apprehension (11)
Astonished (6)
Challenge (4)
Collaborator; partner (4)
Congenial; friendly (7)
Deceived; fooled (7)
Deceiver (9)
Deception (6)
Detestable (6)
Eager to equal or surpass another (7)
Encouraged (7)
Enemies (4)
Facial expression (11)
Flippancy (6)
Forecast (9)
Frank (6)
Go before (7)
Good-natured (7)
Infuriate (10)
Irritable (7)

Lazy; inactive (4)
Listlessness (8)
Madness caused by illness (8)
Nobility; graciousness (11)
Overpower (8)
Payment (10)
Prayers (7)
Presumptuous and insulting in manner or speech (9)
Pretend (7)
Prevent difficulties by effective measures (7)
Read (7)
Revealed (7)
Scheme (8)
Self-righteous (13)
Settling comfortably (10)
Situation; condition (6)
Spitefulness (14)
Tolerate (6)
Turned away (7)
Unreasonable ill temper (9)
Whims (8)
Worry (4)

Wuthering Heights Vocabulary Word Search 3

```
A N N I H I L A T E L P D E T T E B A Q
S S C O R D I A L A V E R T E D D L D N
H A O E N D U R E M S E V H G Q V E E F
A P N W C E L G U P G V F I C G R I T Y
Z P S G D F K I O S Q I R F T E D N S Q
H N P Y U Y R N C E F S E Y V Y E D E X
C J I A S I D Y C O N H T E Z S G I F S
V C R G L E N N C F E S S V N F R G I N
M S E E N L A E D T D R C E T X A N N L
I U D C G L G V I E E A T O E Q D A A X
D S Y Y U I Z R D P L E L T N E A T M J
L C G T L V C N L O R U A L N C T I I S
E E E B H O E P C P R R D R Y H I O T Y
T P O Y P T R X D O E I E E S M O N I V
A T X Y R E P E E P N C S I D M N T G C
I I H O C Q C L S D S T U O Y L S S A V
V B P E H N M A I I W Q R G N A X N T F
B L D Y I J X L D G N Z E I H S D M E W
O E H V J E C G H A H T P G V I W D D M
W F E I G N E D V Q V T A H D E C E I T
```

ABETTED	DESPONDENCY	OBLIGE
AGHAST	DISCERNED	OBVIATE
ALLY	ENDURE	ORISONS
ANNIHILATE	ENSCONCING	PEEVISH
APPALL	EVINCED	PERSEVERED
AVERTED	EXASPERATE	PERUSED
CANDID	FEIGNED	PETULANCE
CONSPIRE	FOES	PLIGHT
CONTRIVE	FRET	PORTENDED
CORDIAL	HYPOCRITE	PRECEDE
DECEIT	IDLE	PRETENSE
DEFY	INDIGNATION	SANGUINE
DEGRADATION	LEVITY	SUSCEPTIBLE
DELIRIUM	MANIFESTED	VANQUISH
DELUDED	MITIGATED	VEXED

Wuthering Heights Vocabulary Word Search 3 Answer Key

```
A  N  N  I  H  I  L  A  T  E  L  P  D  E  T  T  E  B  A
S     C  O  R  D  I  A  L  A  V  E  R  T  E  D        D
   A  O  E  N  D  U  R  E  M  S  E  V           E     E
A     N        E           U  P  V  F        I  R     T
      P  S  G  F        I  O  S     I  R     T  E     S
         P     U  Y  R  N     E     R  E     V  Y  E  E
         I     A  I  D     C  O  N  H  T  E     N  G  F
         R     L  E  N  N     F  E  S  S     N  R  I
      S  E  E  N  L  A  E  D  T  D  R  C  E     A  N
I     U  D  C     L  G     I  E  E  A  T  O  E  D  A  M
D  S  Y        U  I     R  D  P  L  E  L  T  N  E  A  T
L  C     T  L  V  C  N     O  R  U  A  L  N  C  T  I  I
E  E  E  B     O  E  P  C  P  R  R  D  R  Y  H  I  O  T
T  P  O     P  T  R  X  D  O  E  I  E  E  S     O  N  I
A  T     Y  R  E  P  E  E  P  N  C  S  I  D     N  G  C
I  I  H  O  C     C  L  S  D  S  T  U  O        S     A
V  B  P  E     N     A  I  I        Q  R     N  A  N  T
B  L  D        I     X     D  G  N     E  I  H  S  D  E
O  E     V     E           A  H     P  G  V  I        D
F  E  I  G  N  E  D  V              T  A     D  E  C  E  I  T
```

ABETTED	DESPONDENCY	OBLIGE
AGHAST	DISCERNED	OBVIATE
ALLY	ENDURE	ORISONS
ANNIHILATE	ENSCONCING	PEEVISH
APPALL	EVINCED	PERSEVERED
AVERTED	EXASPERATE	PERUSED
CANDID	FEIGNED	PETULANCE
CONSPIRE	FOES	PLIGHT
CONTRIVE	FRET	PORTENDED
CORDIAL	HYPOCRITE	PRECEDE
DECEIT	IDLE	PRETENSE
DEFY	INDIGNATION	SANGUINE
DEGRADATION	LEVITY	SUSCEPTIBLE
DELIRIUM	MANIFESTED	VANQUISH
DELUDED	MITIGATED	VEXED

Wuthering Heights Vocabulary Word Search 4

```
E N S C O N C I N G D E L I C N O C E R
P E C N A N E T N U O C P O A M Q N K M
S A T U R N I N E M T P N P B G Q W J R
D E L U D E D O U R V D P R E C E D E T
S U S C E P T I B L E S N E T E R P H C
O X W E Z H R T D S X C T Z T Y V G N Y
B C L P H I R R C S P H O X E F I I L M
L D W D L T S E I U O S C M D L R L S N
I C G E S U N S N O S I R O P Y A E C H
G G D A O D R S S I T U N Q R E N O T Y
E J H L I W F A O D Q L D K D N C T N
N G U N J O G E L O L N P Y U S I S K D
A M G F E I G N E D A A S R P L S A E D
E M F S S L A I N E T V E I E E G F L J
D V I Y F Z V U C X I K R T C V Y E G H
D E I A B Z E G E E N E H I V I G Y N Q
L F C N B K R N N V G A R H Q T K Z F T
Z G F E C L T A P K R P S X N Y M N Z F
R N P Q I E E S H G A M I T I G A T E D
H K S M X T D K Y C Z M A P P A L L N X
```

ABETTED	DELIRIUM	MITIGATED
AGHAST	DELUDED	OBLIGE
ALLY	EMULOUS	ODIOUS
AMIABLE	ENDURE	ORISONS
APPALL	ENSCONCING	PEEVISH
ASSERTION	EVINCED	PLIGHT
AVERTED	EXPOSTULATING	PRECEDE
CANDID	FEIGNED	PRETENSE
CAPRICES	FOES	RECOMPENSE
CONDESCENDING	FRET	RECONCILED
CONSPIRE	IDLE	SANGUINE
CORDIAL	INDULGENT	SATURNINE
COUNTENANCE	INSOLENCE	SUSCEPTIBLE
DECEIT	LETHARGY	VANQUISH
DEFY	LEVITY	VEXED

Wuthering Heights Vocabulary Word Search 4 Answer Key

ABETTED	DELIRIUM	MITIGATED
AGHAST	DELUDED	OBLIGE
ALLY	EMULOUS	ODIOUS
AMIABLE	ENDURE	ORISONS
APPALL	ENSCONCING	PEEVISH
ASSERTION	EVINCED	PLIGHT
AVERTED	EXPOSTULATING	PRECEDE
CANDID	FEIGNED	PRETENSE
CAPRICES	FOES	RECOMPENSE
CONDESCENDING	FRET	RECONCILED
CONSPIRE	IDLE	SANGUINE
CORDIAL	INDULGENT	SATURNINE
COUNTENANCE	INSOLENCE	SUSCEPTIBLE
DECEIT	LETHARGY	VANQUISH
DEFY	LEVITY	VEXED

Wuthering Heights Vocabulary Crossword 1

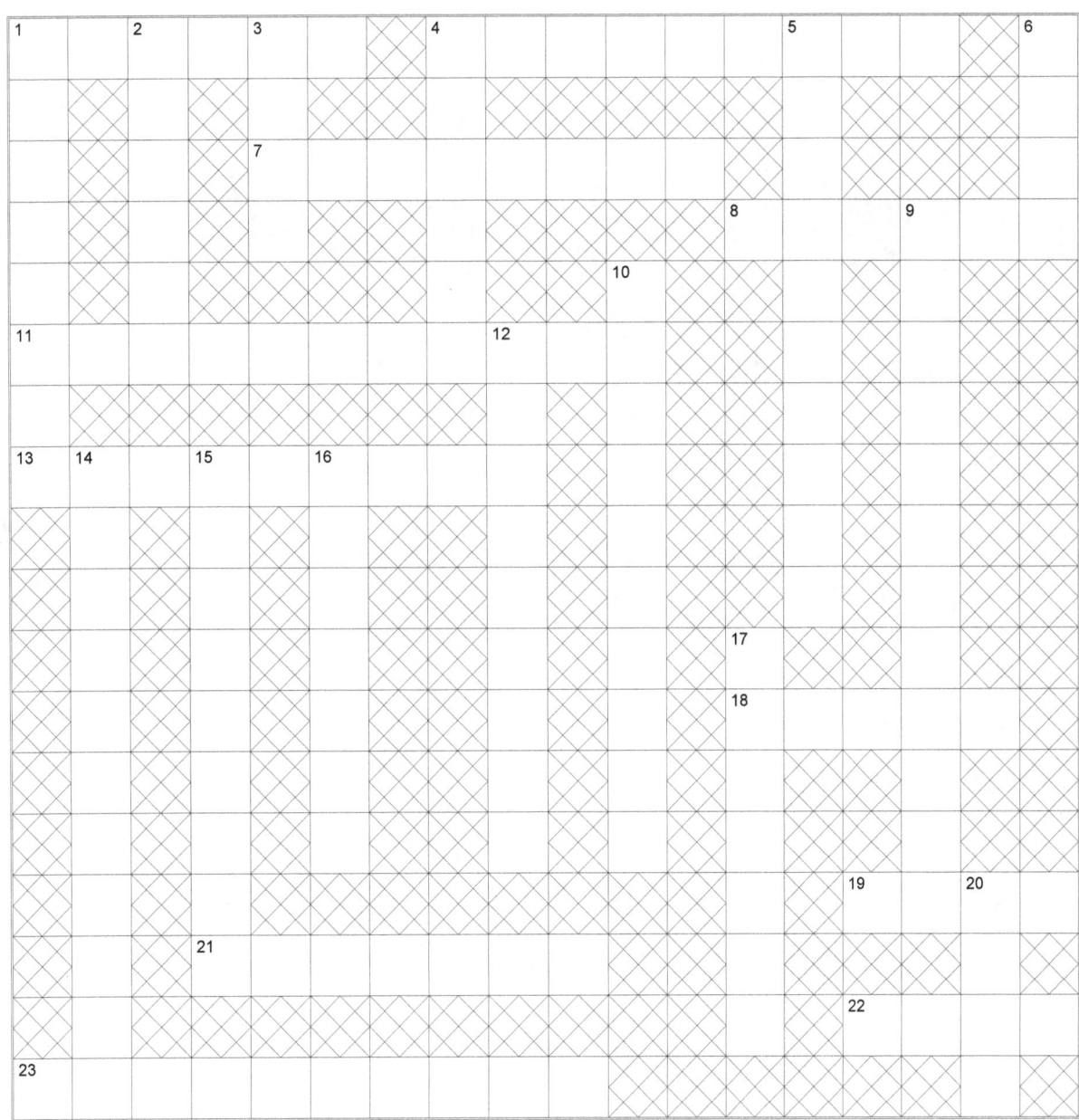

Across
1. Deception
4. Statement
7. Listlessness
8. Flippancy
11. Resentment
13. Moderated
18. Annoyed
19. Challenge
21. Eager to equal or surpass another
22. Worry
23. Persisted

Down
1. Madness caused by illness
2. Frank
3. Lazy; inactive
4. Astonished
5. Intruder
6. Collaborator; partner
9. Impudence
10. Settling comfortably
12. Obliging; lenient
14. Uncontrollable
15. Presumptuous and insulting in manner or speech
16. Turned away
17. Revealed
20. Enemies

Wuthering Heights Vocabulary Crossword 1 Answer Key

	1 D	2 C	3 E	I	T		4 A	S	S	E	R	5 T	I	O	N		6 A
	E		A		D		G					N					L
	L		N	7 L	E	T	H	A	R	G	Y						L
	I		D	E			A					8 L	E	9 V	I	T	Y
	R		I	E			S				10 E		R		M		
11 I	N	D	I	G	N	A	T	12 I	O	N			L		P		
U								N		S			O		E		
13 M	14 I	T	15 I	16 G	A	T	E	D		C			P		R		
	N		N	V				U		O			E		T		
	T		S	E				L		N			R		I		
	R		O	R				G		C		17 E			N		
	A		L	T				E		I		18 V	E	X	E	D	
	C		E	E				N		N		I			N		
	T		N	D				T		G		N			C		
	A		C									C		19 D	E	20 F	Y
	B		21 E	M	U	L	O	U	S			E				O	
	L											D		22 F	R	E	T
23 P	E	R	S	E	V	E	R	E	D							S	

Across
1. Deception
4. Statement
7. Listlessness
8. Flippancy
11. Resentment
13. Moderated
18. Annoyed
19. Challenge
21. Eager to equal or surpass another
22. Worry
23. Persisted

Down
1. Madness caused by illness
2. Frank
3. Lazy; inactive
4. Astonished
5. Intruder
6. Collaborator; partner
9. Impudence
10. Settling comfortably
12. Obliging; lenient
14. Uncontrollable
15. Presumptuous and insulting in manner or speech
16. Turned away
17. Revealed
20. Enemies

Wuthering Heights Vocabulary Crossword 2

Across
- 4. Challenge
- 6. Reasoning to dissuade or correct
- 7. Astonished
- 11. Return
- 17. Lazy; inactive
- 18. Embarrassment
- 21. Annoyed
- 22. Deception
- 23. Frank

Down
- 1. Enemies
- 2. Collaborator; partner
- 3. Energy
- 5. Worry
- 6. Tolerate
- 8. Optimistic
- 9. Scheme
- 10. Presumptuous and insulting in manner or speech
- 12. Apologetic
- 13. Irritable
- 14. Infuriate
- 15. Devise; find a way
- 16. Eager to equal or surpass another
- 19. Obliging; lenient
- 20. Go before

Wuthering Heights Vocabulary Crossword 2 Answer Key

Across
- 4. Challenge
- 6. Reasoning to dissuade or correct
- 7. Astonished
- 11. Return
- 17. Lazy; inactive
- 18. Embarrassment
- 21. Annoyed
- 22. Deception
- 23. Frank

Down
- 1. Enemies
- 2. Collaborator; partner
- 3. Energy
- 5. Worry
- 6. Tolerate
- 8. Optimistic
- 9. Scheme
- 10. Presumptuous and insulting in manner or speech
- 12. Apologetic
- 13. Irritable
- 14. Infuriate
- 15. Devise; find a way
- 16. Eager to equal or surpass another
- 19. Obliging; lenient
- 20. Go before

Wuthering Heights Vocabulary Crossword 3

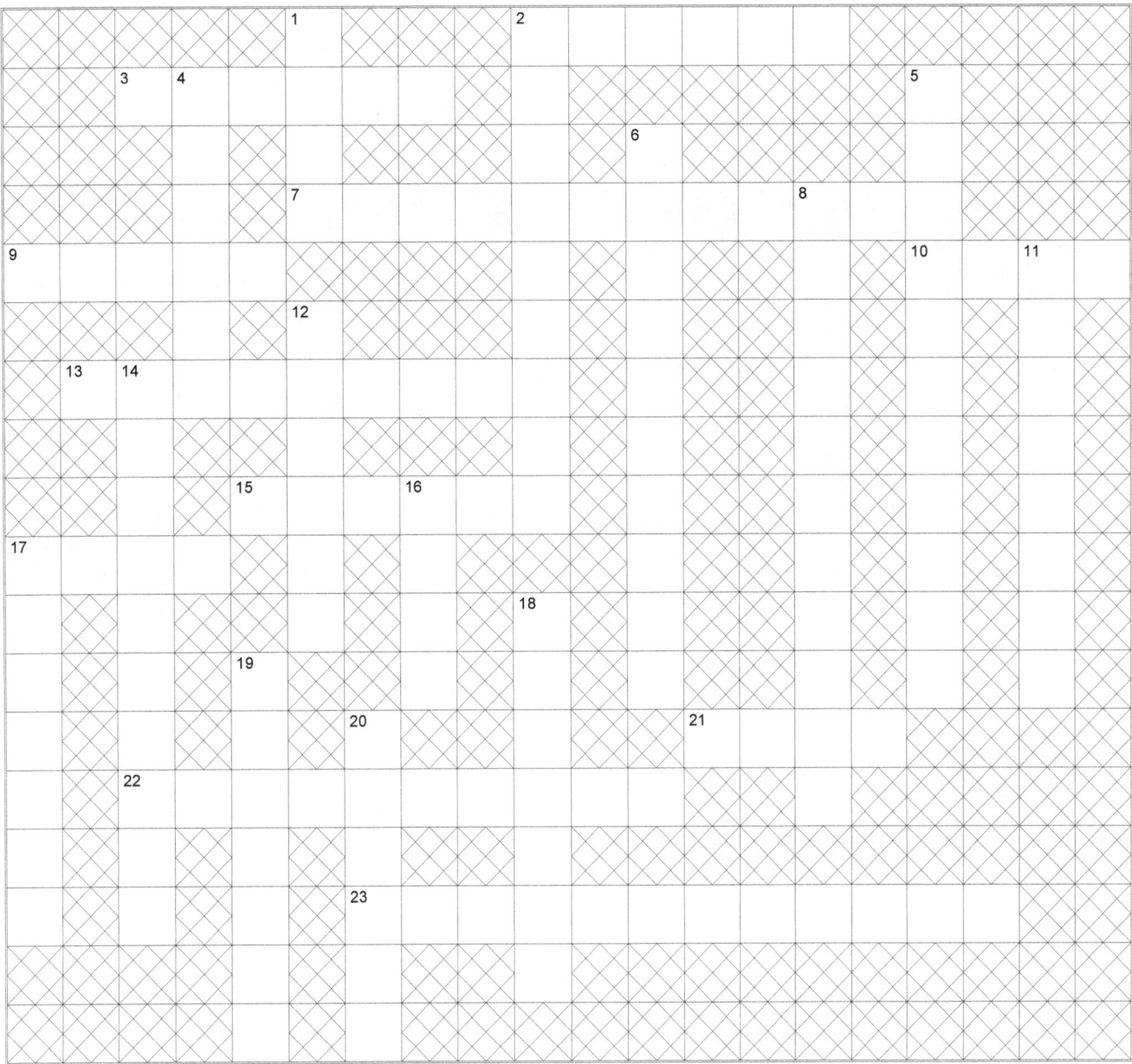

Across
 2. Situation; condition
 3. Detestable
 7. Inspecting
 9. Annoyed
10. Lazy; inactive
13. Moderated
15. Frank
17. Worry
21. Collaborator; partner
22. Persisted
23. Impudence

Down
 1. Enemies
 2. Forecast
 4. Deception
 5. Thoughts
 6. Settling comfortably
 8. Uncontrollable
11. Listlessness
12. Astonished
14. Intruder
16. Challenge
17. Pretend
18. Turned away
19. Read
20. Flippancy

Wuthering Heights Vocabulary Crossword 3 Answer Key

```
            1 F         2 P  L  I  G  H  T
      3 O  4 D  I  O  U  S  O              5 C
            E     E        6 E              O
            C   7 S  C  R  U  T  I  N  I  Z  8 I  N  G
9 V  E  X  E  D              E        S        10 I  D  11 L
            I   12 A           N        C        T     E
   13 M 14 I  T  I  G  A  T  E  D     O        R     A     T
         N        H              E        N        A     H
         T    15 C  A  N  16 D  I  D     C        C     I     A
17 F  R  E  T     S     E           I        T     O     R
E         R        T     18 F  A        N        A     N     G
I         L    19 P     Y  V        G        B     S     Y
G         O     E     20 L     E        21 A  L  L  Y
N       22 P  E  R  S  E  V  E  R  E  D        E
E         E        U        V              T
D         R        S    23 I  M  P  E  R  T  I  N  E  N  C  E
                   E        T              D
                   D        Y
```

Across
2. Situation; condition
3. Detestable
7. Inspecting
9. Annoyed
10. Lazy; inactive
13. Moderated
15. Frank
17. Worry
21. Collaborator; partner
22. Persisted
23. Impudence

Down
1. Enemies
2. Forecast
4. Deception
5. Thoughts
6. Settling comfortably
8. Uncontrollable
11. Listlessness
12. Astonished
14. Intruder
16. Challenge
17. Pretend
18. Turned away
19. Read
20. Flippancy

Wuthering Heights Vocabulary Crossword 4

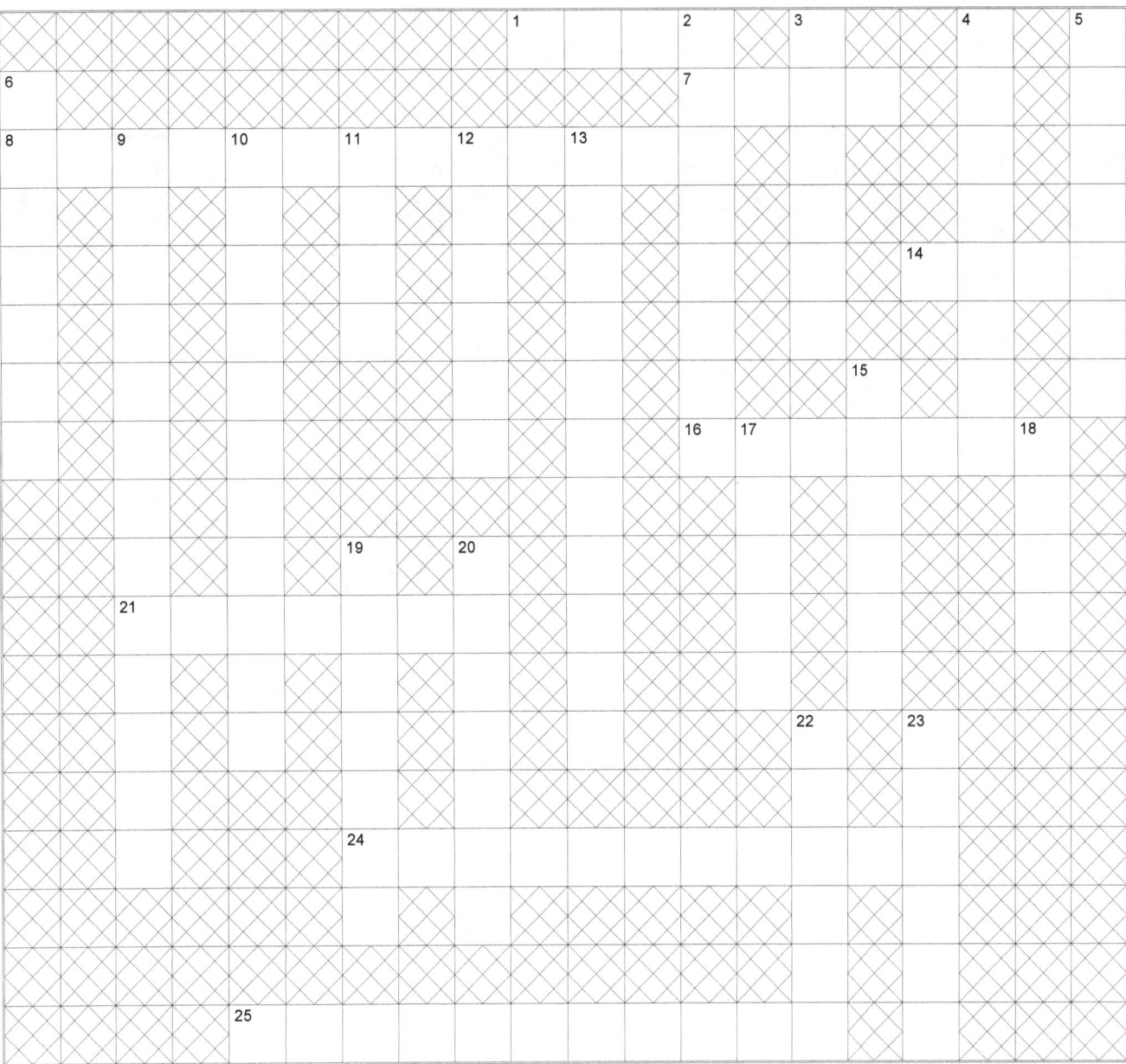

Across
1. Enemies
7. Collaborator; partner
8. Embarrassment
14. Worry
16. Revealed
21. Good-natured
24. Apprehension
25. Thoughts

Down
2. Optimistic
3. Situation; condition
4. Apologetic
5. Encouraged
6. Eager to equal or surpass another
9. Return
10. Resentment
11. Lazy; inactive
12. Astonished
13. Uncontrollable
15. Tolerate
17. Annoyed
18. Challenge
19. Prevent difficulties by effective measures
20. Pretend
22. Detestable
23. Frank

101 Copyright 2005 Teacher's Pet Publications

Wuthering Heights Vocabulary Crossword 4 Answer Key

						¹F	O	E	²S		³P			⁴C		⁵A
⁶E									⁷A	L	L	Y		O		B
⁸M	⁹O	R	¹⁰T	I	¹¹F	I	¹²C	A	¹³T	I	O	N		N		E
U	E		N		D		G		N		G			T		T
L	C		D		L		H		T		U		¹⁴F	R	E	T
O	I		I		E		A		R		I			I		E
U	P		G				S		A		N		¹⁵E		T	D
S	R		N				T		C		¹⁶E	¹⁷V	I	N	C	¹⁸E
	O		A						T			E		D		E
	C		T			¹⁹O		²⁰F			A		X		U		F
	²¹A	M	I	A	B	L	E		B			E		R		Y
	T		O		V		I		L			D		E		
	I		N		I		G		E			²²O		²³C		
	O				A		N					D		A		
	N			²⁴T	R	E	P	I	D	A	T	I	O	N		
				E		D						O		D		
												U		I		
			²⁵C	O	G	I	T	A	T	I	O	N	S		D	

Across
1. Enemies
7. Collaborator; partner
8. Embarrassment
14. Worry
16. Revealed
21. Good-natured
24. Apprehension
25. Thoughts

Down
2. Optimistic
3. Situation; condition
4. Apologetic
5. Encouraged
6. Eager to equal or surpass another
9. Return
10. Resentment
11. Lazy; inactive
12. Astonished
13. Uncontrollable
15. Tolerate
17. Annoyed
18. Challenge
19. Prevent difficulties by effective measures
20. Pretend
22. Detestable
23. Frank

Wuthering Heights Vocabulary Juggle Letters 1

1. IDIAMTETG = 1. _____
   Moderated

2. EDIL = 2. _____
   Lazy; inactive

3. GDNDOEIENNCSC = 3. _____
   Patronizing

4. CNLERODECI = 4. _____
   Reunited

5. DAREVTE = 5. _____
   Turned away

6. COOIANTNMSUSI = 6. _____
   Self-righteous

7. TEALCNEUP = 7. _____
   Unreasonable ill temper

8. AOVETIB = 8. _____
   Prevent difficulties by effective measures

9. LXETPSGONAUTI = 9. _____
   Reasoning to dissuade or correct

10. TANIURNES =10. _____
    Sullen

11. NTSEEPER =11. _____
    False appearance or action

12. QIUASVNH =12. _____
    Overpower

13. TDEAROANGID =13. _____
    Disgrace

14. ECORTVIN =14. _____
    Devise; find a way

15. ENROCTIT =15. _____
    Apologetic

Wuthering Heights Vocabulary Juggle Letters 1 Answer Key

1. IDIAMTETG = 1. MITIGATED
   Moderated

2. EDIL = 2. IDLE
   Lazy; inactive

3. GDNDOEIENNCSC = 3. CONDESCENDING
   Patronizing

4. CNLERODECI = 4. RECONCILED
   Reunited

5. DAREVTE = 5. AVERTED
   Turned away

6. COOIANTNMSUSI = 6. SANCTIMONIOUS
   Self-righteous

7. TEALCNEUP = 7. PETULANCE
   Unreasonable ill temper

8. AOVETIB = 8. OBVIATE
   Prevent difficulties by effective measures

9. LXETPSGONAUTI = 9. EXPOSTULATING
   Reasoning to dissuade or correct

10. TANIURNES = 10. SATURNINE
    Sullen

11. NTSEEPER = 11. PRETENSE
    False appearance or action

12. QIUASVNH = 12. VANQUISH
    Overpower

13. TDEAROANGID = 13. DEGRADATION
    Disgrace

14. ECORTVIN = 14. CONTRIVE
    Devise; find a way

15. ENROCTIT = 15. CONTRITE
    Apologetic

Wuthering Heights Vocabulary Juggle Letters 2

1. LIDAORC = 1. _____
   Congenial; friendly

2. ETNACNUOCEN = 2. _____
   Facial expression

3. TABEIVO = 3. _____
   Prevent difficulties by effective measures

4. DEXEV = 4. _____
   Annoyed

5. IVAYTVIC = 5. _____
   Energy

6. DNAMNOTOII = 6. _____
   Advice

7. OPDIIATTNER = 7. _____
   Apprehension

8. MMATYNANIGI = 8. _____
   Nobility; graciousness

9. DVINCEE = 9. _____
   Revealed

10. RTFE = 10. _____
    Worry

11. QEICUDSEAC = 11. _____
    Consented

12. CRTCDATNIO = 12. _____
    Dispute; oppose

13. EJCENUORTC = 13. _____
    Suppose

14. LDCOIEENCR = 14. _____
    Reunited

15. NEDFGEI = 15. _____
    Pretend

Wuthering Heights Vocabulary Juggle Letters 2 Answer Key

1. LIDAORC = 1. CORDIAL
Congenial; friendly

2. ETNACNUOCEN = 2. COUNTENANCE
Facial expression

3. TABEIVO = 3. OBVIATE
Prevent difficulties by effective measures

4. DEXEV = 4. VEXED
Annoyed

5. IVAYTVIC = 5. VIVACITY
Energy

6. DNAMNOTOII = 6. ADMONITION
Advice

7. OPDIIATTNER = 7. TREPIDATION
Apprehension

8. MMATYNANIGI = 8. MAGNANIMITY
Nobility; graciousness

9. DVINCEE = 9. EVINCED
Revealed

10. RTFE = 10. FRET
Worry

11. QEICUDSEAC = 11. ACQUIESCED
Consented

12. CRTCDATNIO = 12. CONTRADICT
Dispute; oppose

13. EJCENUORTC = 13. CONJECTURE
Suppose

14. LDCOIEENCR = 14. RECONCILED
Reunited

15. NEDFGEI = 15. FEIGNED
Pretend

Wuthering Heights Vocabulary Juggle Letters 3

1. DCDEENINGSNOC = 1. _____
   Patronizing

2. IDIIONANGNT = 2. _____
   Resentment

3. TIVRNCOE = 3. _____
   Devise; find a way

4. LPAPAL = 4. _____
   Dismay

5. CSENOEDYDNP = 5. _____
   Discouragement

6. ABOTVIE = 6. _____
   Prevent difficulties by effective measures

7. LBEMIAA = 7. _____
   Good-natured

8. EDTGNAAIDRO = 8. _____
   Disgrace

9. ITACOMITRINOF = 9. _____
   Embarrassment

10. ETFR = 10. _____
    Worry

11. ISHPEEV = 11. _____
    Irritable

12. VDIEENC = 12. _____
    Revealed

13. EVSEEEDRPR = 13. _____
    Persisted

14. UEEPSRD = 14. _____
    Read

15. OCTERNIT = 15. _____
    Apologetic

Wuthering Heights Vocabulary Juggle Letters 3 Answer Key

1. DCDEENINGSNOC = 1. CONDESCENDING
   Patronizing

2. IDIIONANGNT = 2. INDIGNATION
   Resentment

3. TIVRNCOE = 3. CONTRIVE
   Devise; find a way

4. LPAPAL = 4. APPALL
   Dismay

5. CSENOEDYDNP = 5. DESPONDENCY
   Discouragement

6. ABOTVIE = 6. OBVIATE
   Prevent difficulties by effective measures

7. LBEMIAA = 7. AMIABLE
   Good-natured

8. EDTGNAAIDRO = 8. DEGRADATION
   Disgrace

9. ITACOMITRINOF = 9. MORTIFICATION
   Embarrassment

10. ETFR = 10. FRET
    Worry

11. ISHPEEV = 11. PEEVISH
    Irritable

12. VDIEENC = 12. EVINCED
    Revealed

13. EVSEEEDRPR = 13. PERSEVERED
    Persisted

14. UEEPSRD = 14. PERUSED
    Read

15. OCTERNIT = 15. CONTRITE
    Apologetic

Wuthering Heights Vocabulary Juggle Letters 4

1. ECTRNITO = 1. _____
Apologetic

2. ITCZNIISURGN = 2. _____
Inspecting

3. ECEORNDCLI = 3. _____
Reunited

4. EERCITINNEPM = 4. _____
Impudence

5. SOIORNS = 5. _____
Prayers

6. ILEBOG = 6. _____
Accommodate

7. ICIAYVVT = 7. _____
Energy

8. ULNIGETDN = 8. _____
Obliging; lenient

9. LCTEUNPEA = 9. _____
Unreasonable ill temper

10. PCLSYOMURO =10. _____
Mandatory; involuntary

11. ITRAOYLD =11. _____
Cleverly; deftly

12. NPOYPSTEIR =12. _____
Tendency

13. REOUCENTJC =13. _____
Suppose

14. EDINFEG =14. _____
Pretend

15. TFRE =15. _____
Worry

Wuthering Heights Vocabulary Juggle Letters 4 Answer Key

1. ECTRNITO = 1. CONTRITE
   Apologetic

2. ITCZNIISURGN = 2. SCRUTINIZING
   Inspecting

3. ECEORNDCLI = 3. RECONCILED
   Reunited

4. EERCITINNEPM = 4. IMPERTINENCE
   Impudence

5. SOIORNS = 5. ORISONS
   Prayers

6. ILEBOG = 6. OBLIGE
   Accommodate

7. ICIAYVVT = 7. VIVACITY
   Energy

8. ULNIGETDN = 8. INDULGENT
   Obliging; lenient

9. LCTEUNPEA = 9. PETULANCE
   Unreasonable ill temper

10. PCLSYOMURO = 10. COMPULSORY
    Mandatory; involuntary

11. ITRAOYLD = 11. ADROITLY
    Cleverly; deftly

12. NPOYPSTEIR = 12. PROPENSITY
    Tendency

13. REOUCENTJC = 13. CONJECTURE
    Suppose

14. EDINFEG = 14. FEIGNED
    Pretend

15. TFRE = 15. FRET
    Worry

ABETTED	Encouraged
ACQUIESCED	Consented
ADMONITION	Advice
ADROITLY	Cleverly; deftly
AFFIRMING	Asserting; maintaining
AGHAST	Astonished
ALLY	Collaborator; partner

AMIABLE	Good-natured
ANNIHILATE	Obliterate
APPALL	Dismay
ASSERTION	Statement
AVERTED	Turned away
CANDID	Frank
CAPRICES	Whims

COGITATIONS	Thoughts
COMPULSORY	Mandatory; involuntary
CONDESCENDING	Patronizing
CONJECTURE	Suppose
CONSPIRE	Scheme
CONTRADICT	Dispute; oppose
CONTRITE	Apologetic

CONTRIVE	Devise; find a way
CORDIAL	Congenial; friendly
COUNTENANCE	Facial expression
DECEIT	Deception
DEFY	Challenge
DEGRADATION	Disgrace
DELIRIUM	Madness caused by illness

DELUDED	Deceived; fooled
DESPONDENCY	Discouragement
DISCERNED	Perceived
EMULOUS	Eager to equal or surpass another
ENDURE	Tolerate
ENSCONCING	Settling comfortably
EVINCED	Revealed

EXASPERATE	Infuriate
EXPOSTULATING	Reasoning to dissuade or correct
FEIGNED	Pretend
FOES	Enemies
FRET	Worry
HYPOCRITE	Deceiver
IDLE	Lazy; inactive

IMPERTINENCE	Impudence
INDIGNATION	Resentment
INDULGENT	Obliging; lenient
INSOLENCE	Presumptuous and insulting in manner or speech
INTERLOPER	Intruder
INTRACTABLE	Uncontrollable
LETHARGY	Listlessness

LEVITY	Flippancy
MAGNANIMITY	Nobility; graciousness
MANIFESTED	Exhibited
MISANTHROPIST	Person who hates mankind
MITIGATED	Moderated
MORTIFICATION	Embarrassment
OBLIGE	Accommodate

OBVIATE	Prevent difficulties by effective measures
ODIOUS	Detestable
ORISONS	Prayers
PEEVISH	Irritable
PERPETUAL	Continuous; endless
PERSEVERED	Persisted
PERUSED	Read

PETULANCE	Unreasonable ill temper
PLIGHT	Situation; condition
PORTENDED	Forecast
PRECEDE	Go before
PRETENSE	False appearance or action
PROPENSITY	Tendency
PROVINCIALISMS	Manners unfashionable or unsophisticated

RECIPROCATION	Return
RECOMPENSE	Payment
RECONCILED	Reunited
SANCTIMONIOUS	Self-righteous
SANGUINE	Optimistic
SATURNINE	Sullen
SCRUTINIZING	Inspecting

SUSCEPTIBLE	Vulnerable
TREPIDATION	Apprehension
VANQUISH	Overpower
VEXED	Annoyed
VINDICTIVENESS	Spitefulness
VIVACITY	Energy

Wuthering Heights Vocabulary

PLIGHT	MISANTHROPIST	COMPULSORY	VANQUISH	SANCTIMONIOUS
ODIOUS	CAPRICES	LETHARGY	HYPOCRITE	LEVITY
ADROITLY	SANGUINE	FREE SPACE	CONSPIRE	DISCERNED
EXASPERATE	FEIGNED	PRECEDE	DESPONDENCY	CANDID
AGHAST	ALLY	OBVIATE	FOES	INTERLOPER

Wuthering Heights Vocabulary

RECOMPENSE	ASSERTION	EVINCED	SATURNINE	EXPOSTULATING
CONTRITE	VEXED	SUSCEPTIBLE	INDULGENT	INDIGNATION
PRETENSE	AVERTED	FREE SPACE	PORTENDED	COGITATIONS
ANNIHILATE	PROVINCIALISMS	ABETTED	VIVACITY	RECIPROCATION
INSOLENCE	ADMONITION	CONDESCENDING	AFFIRMING	PROPENSITY

Wuthering Heights Vocabulary

ADMONITION	ENDURE	DEFY	LEVITY	ABETTED
MORTIFICATION	CONTRITE	CORDIAL	HYPOCRITE	PETULANCE
PLIGHT	MISANTHROPIST	FREE SPACE	FOES	AFFIRMING
CONTRADICT	CAPRICES	SANCTIMONIOUS	RECIPROCATION	SCRUTINIZING
PEEVISH	ORISONS	DELIRIUM	AMIABLE	PRETENSE

Wuthering Heights Vocabulary

PERUSED	AVERTED	IMPERTINENCE	IDLE	PROVINCIALISMS
APPALL	LETHARGY	MITIGATED	ENSCONCING	PORTENDED
EXASPERATE	VIVACITY	FREE SPACE	EMULOUS	ADROITLY
SANGUINE	DELUDED	PROPENSITY	PRECEDE	COMPULSORY
ACQUIESCED	OBVIATE	AGHAST	COUNTENANCE	ALLY

Wuthering Heights Vocabulary

DELIRIUM	AVERTED	FRET	SANGUINE	CONSPIRE
ANNIHILATE	AMIABLE	RECIPROCATION	DEFY	EXPOSTULATING
TREPIDATION	CONDESCENDING	FREE SPACE	DELUDED	MITIGATED
DECEIT	MAGNANIMITY	PLIGHT	CONTRADICT	INDULGENT
SATURNINE	FEIGNED	EVINCED	ENSCONCING	ACQUIESCED

Wuthering Heights Vocabulary

ASSERTION	ODIOUS	INDIGNATION	PERSEVERED	DEGRADATION
FOES	MISANTHROPIST	MANIFESTED	ORISONS	PRECEDE
PEEVISH	EXASPERATE	FREE SPACE	ENDURE	PORTENDED
INTRACTABLE	VEXED	IDLE	RECOMPENSE	CONTRIVE
ABETTED	PERPETUAL	IMPERTINENCE	DESPONDENCY	CONJECTURE

Wuthering Heights Vocabulary

AVERTED	MORTIFICATION	ACQUIESCED	INDIGNATION	EMULOUS
AGHAST	MAGNANIMITY	PROPENSITY	PLIGHT	ABETTED
CONTRIVE	PEEVISH	FREE SPACE	PERSEVERED	INTRACTABLE
MISANTHROPIST	DELIRIUM	AMIABLE	DEFY	CONDESCENDING
SUSCEPTIBLE	INSOLENCE	DISCERNED	RECONCILED	VEXED

Wuthering Heights Vocabulary

PERUSED	SATURNINE	CORDIAL	FEIGNED	LETHARGY
PERPETUAL	IDLE	CONSPIRE	COMPULSORY	VIVACITY
ANNIHILATE	ALLY	FREE SPACE	TREPIDATION	CONJECTURE
RECOMPENSE	RECIPROCATION	INTERLOPER	CAPRICES	FRET
CONTRITE	HYPOCRITE	ADROITLY	MITIGATED	AFFIRMING

Wuthering Heights Vocabulary

ADROITLY	INTRACTABLE	CANDID	IMPERTINENCE	COGITATIONS
AGHAST	DISCERNED	EMULOUS	ENSCONCING	EXPOSTULATING
DELIRIUM	OBLIGE	FREE SPACE	PRETENSE	MITIGATED
PRECEDE	PETULANCE	CONJECTURE	PORTENDED	ENDURE
INTERLOPER	MANIFESTED	ABETTED	FOES	INSOLENCE

Wuthering Heights Vocabulary

INDIGNATION	PERSEVERED	FRET	ADMONITION	TREPIDATION
VIVACITY	SANGUINE	COMPULSORY	PEEVISH	ANNIHILATE
ORISONS	MISANTHROPIST	FREE SPACE	DEGRADATION	AVERTED
APPALL	LEVITY	ALLY	CONSPIRE	DEFY
CONTRADICT	EVINCED	AMIABLE	SATURNINE	AFFIRMING

Wuthering Heights Vocabulary

CONTRIVE	AGHAST	RECONCILED	LEVITY	CORDIAL
INDIGNATION	INDULGENT	PORTENDED	CAPRICES	COGITATIONS
SANCTIMONIOUS	PLIGHT	FREE SPACE	INTRACTABLE	OBVIATE
COUNTENANCE	CONTRITE	ORISONS	DECEIT	EXPOSTULATING
PRETENSE	ENDURE	CONSPIRE	AVERTED	EVINCED

Wuthering Heights Vocabulary

VIVACITY	FRET	MITIGATED	CONDESCENDING	ADMONITION
MISANTHROPIST	INTERLOPER	VINDICTIVENESS	COMPULSORY	LETHARGY
ALLY	RECIPROCATION	FREE SPACE	PROPENSITY	AFFIRMING
SCRUTINIZING	RECOMPENSE	PERPETUAL	APPALL	SUSCEPTIBLE
CONTRADICT	ANNIHILATE	MAGNANIMITY	INSOLENCE	EXASPERATE

Wuthering Heights Vocabulary

RECIPROCATION	COUNTENANCE	CAPRICES	MORTIFICATION	PRECEDE
SUSCEPTIBLE	IDLE	ANNIHILATE	CONTRITE	COGITATIONS
INDULGENT	DECEIT	FREE SPACE	FOES	AFFIRMING
AGHAST	VIVACITY	ENDURE	DEGRADATION	INSOLENCE
ODIOUS	ORISONS	VEXED	ADMONITION	OBLIGE

Wuthering Heights Vocabulary

FRET	CANDID	SANGUINE	ALLY	ENSCONCING
OBVIATE	LETHARGY	ABETTED	RECOMPENSE	SANCTIMONIOUS
SCRUTINIZING	PORTENDED	FREE SPACE	CONJECTURE	ADROITLY
CONDESCENDING	PROPENSITY	APPALL	PROVINCIALISMS	DESPONDENCY
MISANTHROPIST	ACQUIESCED	TREPIDATION	MITIGATED	EXPOSTULATING

Wuthering Heights Vocabulary

DEGRADATION	SANGUINE	FEIGNED	EMULOUS	VIVACITY
PERUSED	SUSCEPTIBLE	EXASPERATE	CONDESCENDING	PERSEVERED
FRET	MANIFESTED	FREE SPACE	INSOLENCE	ABETTED
MISANTHROPIST	MORTIFICATION	DESPONDENCY	PROVINCIALISMS	LETHARGY
SANCTIMONIOUS	DELUDED	INDULGENT	IDLE	CONTRADICT

Wuthering Heights Vocabulary

COGITATIONS	PROPENSITY	INDIGNATION	APPALL	TREPIDATION
RECIPROCATION	MITIGATED	ASSERTION	ANNIHILATE	EVINCED
FOES	AGHAST	FREE SPACE	PORTENDED	DELIRIUM
OBVIATE	DEFY	ADROITLY	CAPRICES	EXPOSTULATING
INTERLOPER	SCRUTINIZING	COMPULSORY	INTRACTABLE	HYPOCRITE

Wuthering Heights Vocabulary

MAGNANIMITY	DELUDED	PERUSED	INSOLENCE	RECONCILED
ALLY	AGHAST	PETULANCE	SATURNINE	IDLE
OBVIATE	HYPOCRITE	FREE SPACE	IMPERTINENCE	SCRUTINIZING
CONTRADICT	FOES	DELIRIUM	MITIGATED	MISANTHROPIST
EMULOUS	COMPULSORY	VEXED	APPALL	CAPRICES

Wuthering Heights Vocabulary

PRETENSE	CONTRIVE	RECIPROCATION	VINDICTIVENESS	OBLIGE
ABETTED	SUSCEPTIBLE	MANIFESTED	EXASPERATE	VANQUISH
INDULGENT	INTERLOPER	FREE SPACE	SANGUINE	AFFIRMING
SANCTIMONIOUS	ORISONS	PERSEVERED	ADMONITION	FEIGNED
DEFY	VIVACITY	COUNTENANCE	ADROITLY	AVERTED

Wuthering Heights Vocabulary

DESPONDENCY	PRECEDE	ORISONS	ADROITLY	RECOMPENSE
LETHARGY	EMULOUS	PRETENSE	CONJECTURE	ASSERTION
INTRACTABLE	PERUSED	FREE SPACE	VIVACITY	SCRUTINIZING
INDIGNATION	PROVINCIALISMS	DELUDED	PEEVISH	ANNIHILATE
SANCTIMONIOUS	APPALL	EXPOSTULATING	FOES	VEXED

Wuthering Heights Vocabulary

OBLIGE	EXASPERATE	MANIFESTED	PETULANCE	AVERTED
CAPRICES	AMIABLE	SATURNINE	CONTRADICT	AFFIRMING
CORDIAL	MAGNANIMITY	FREE SPACE	HYPOCRITE	ENSCONCING
COMPULSORY	IMPERTINENCE	FRET	PROPENSITY	DEFY
MISANTHROPIST	INSOLENCE	CONTRITE	RECONCILED	DEGRADATION

Wuthering Heights Vocabulary

CORDIAL	VIVACITY	DECEIT	COMPULSORY	INSOLENCE
SANCTIMONIOUS	ASSERTION	DEGRADATION	APPALL	CONTRITE
CONSPIRE	CONJECTURE	FREE SPACE	LETHARGY	ADMONITION
EXPOSTULATING	DELUDED	SANGUINE	DEFY	ODIOUS
AGHAST	FEIGNED	SUSCEPTIBLE	ADROITLY	AVERTED

Wuthering Heights Vocabulary

VEXED	PERSEVERED	FOES	ACQUIESCED	INTRACTABLE
RECIPROCATION	PRECEDE	PROVINCIALISMS	INDIGNATION	DELIRIUM
IDLE	CONTRADICT	FREE SPACE	CANDID	VANQUISH
MAGNANIMITY	RECONCILED	PROPENSITY	ENSCONCING	ORISONS
ALLY	DESPONDENCY	CONDESCENDING	PERUSED	CAPRICES

Wuthering Heights Vocabulary

VINDICTIVENESS	PERUSED	ASSERTION	INSOLENCE	LETHARGY
MORTIFICATION	MISANTHROPIST	ACQUIESCED	IDLE	CONTRIVE
AMIABLE	PRETENSE	FREE SPACE	EMULOUS	ENSCONCING
INTERLOPER	RECOMPENSE	RECIPROCATION	CORDIAL	TREPIDATION
ADROITLY	MITIGATED	RECONCILED	PLIGHT	ODIOUS

Wuthering Heights Vocabulary

AVERTED	PERSEVERED	CANDID	DELIRIUM	VANQUISH
DELUDED	VIVACITY	COGITATIONS	CONDESCENDING	DEGRADATION
FEIGNED	ALLY	FREE SPACE	PORTENDED	DEFY
MANIFESTED	COUNTENANCE	AFFIRMING	CAPRICES	APPALL
EXASPERATE	ENDURE	CONJECTURE	EVINCED	ADMONITION

Wuthering Heights Vocabulary

PRECEDE	FOES	LETHARGY	CONJECTURE	DISCERNED
ABETTED	PERPETUAL	MITIGATED	PROPENSITY	EXPOSTULATING
VEXED	RECONCILED	FREE SPACE	COUNTENANCE	RECOMPENSE
MISANTHROPIST	ACQUIESCED	PETULANCE	ANNIHILATE	EMULOUS
PEEVISH	CONDESCENDING	OBLIGE	FEIGNED	APPALL

Wuthering Heights Vocabulary

ALLY	VIVACITY	AVERTED	CONTRIVE	CONTRADICT
AGHAST	EVINCED	INDULGENT	DECEIT	CANDID
FRET	ORISONS	FREE SPACE	EXASPERATE	ENDURE
SUSCEPTIBLE	MANIFESTED	IDLE	CONSPIRE	AFFIRMING
PERSEVERED	RECIPROCATION	HYPOCRITE	MORTIFICATION	COMPULSORY

Wuthering Heights Vocabulary

PROVINCIALISMS	COGITATIONS	ADROITLY	INSOLENCE	MAGNANIMITY
AFFIRMING	OBLIGE	EXPOSTULATING	CONTRADICT	PRETENSE
TREPIDATION	INTERLOPER	FREE SPACE	ASSERTION	APPALL
ANNIHILATE	PLIGHT	CONDESCENDING	SUSCEPTIBLE	ORISONS
ALLY	CONTRITE	ENDURE	AMIABLE	EVINCED

Wuthering Heights Vocabulary

PORTENDED	IDLE	MORTIFICATION	INDULGENT	LEVITY
LETHARGY	DELIRIUM	SANCTIMONIOUS	IMPERTINENCE	ACQUIESCED
AGHAST	VIVACITY	FREE SPACE	SATURNINE	SANGUINE
COMPULSORY	MANIFESTED	RECIPROCATION	COUNTENANCE	DEGRADATION
PERUSED	DISCERNED	SCRUTINIZING	ADMONITION	CORDIAL

Wuthering Heights Vocabulary

INTRACTABLE	PORTENDED	VINDICTIVENESS	EMULOUS	INTERLOPER
AMIABLE	SUSCEPTIBLE	PROVINCIALISMS	ALLY	MANIFESTED
ABETTED	INDULGENT	FREE SPACE	SANCTIMONIOUS	COMPULSORY
AFFIRMING	ADROITLY	ACQUIESCED	CONTRIVE	EXPOSTULATING
PRECEDE	COGITATIONS	CONTRADICT	CAPRICES	IMPERTINENCE

Wuthering Heights Vocabulary

TREPIDATION	PROPENSITY	CORDIAL	HYPOCRITE	ASSERTION
DESPONDENCY	PEEVISH	MISANTHROPIST	SANGUINE	PERPETUAL
DELIRIUM	PETULANCE	FREE SPACE	EXASPERATE	OBLIGE
DEFY	DELUDED	FEIGNED	FRET	PERSEVERED
MITIGATED	ODIOUS	DEGRADATION	RECOMPENSE	PLIGHT

Wuthering Heights Vocabulary

SATURNINE	CONJECTURE	EMULOUS	INTERLOPER	MAGNANIMITY
ODIOUS	CONTRIVE	ASSERTION	OBLIGE	VEXED
AFFIRMING	CONTRITE	FREE SPACE	DEGRADATION	LETHARGY
AVERTED	INSOLENCE	AMIABLE	ACQUIESCED	DISCERNED
ANNIHILATE	APPALL	PROVINCIALISMS	EXPOSTULATING	HYPOCRITE

Wuthering Heights Vocabulary

VINDICTIVENESS	RECONCILED	CONSPIRE	LEVITY	RECIPROCATION
COMPULSORY	SCRUTINIZING	PORTENDED	AGHAST	SANCTIMONIOUS
PEEVISH	CORDIAL	FREE SPACE	FRET	PERSEVERED
ENDURE	VANQUISH	MORTIFICATION	ADROITLY	ENSCONCING
PRECEDE	SANGUINE	INDULGENT	EVINCED	DELUDED

www.ingramcontent.com/pod-product-compliance
Lightning Source LLC
LaVergne TN
LVHW081538060526
838200LV00048B/2122